SAVING OUR SONS

Strategies and Advice for the Parents of Afrikan Teenage Sons

by

Paul Ifayomi Grant

To Tomiko & Opare
May the Creator bless you
Best Wishes

Navig8or Press, Nottingham, United Kingdom
www.houseofknowledge.org.uk

Published by Navig8or Press
Unit 8
All Saints Centre
Raleigh Street
Nottingham
NG7 4DL
United Kingdom

Cover Layout by Jeremy Prince 3PD design

British Library Cataloguing in Publication Data
A catalogue record for this book is available from the British Library

ISBN 0-9545529-2-X

Printed and bound by Tandem Press
www.tandempress.com

This book is dedicated to

The Creator

My positive female Ancestors
My positive male Ancestors

My son Jawanza Kwesi Grant

All the positive sons of Afrika

All the wonderful women and girls
who have inspired me along my path

To all who struggle for justice

"Black Power is a doctrine about black people, for black people, preached by black people. I'm putting it to my black brothers and sisters that the color of our skins is the most fundamental thing about us. I could have chosen to talk about people of the same island, or the same religion, or the same class – but instead I have chosen skin color as essentially the most binding factor in our world. In so doing, I am not saying that is the way things ought to be. I am simply recognizing the real world – that is the way things are. Under different circumstances, it would have been nice to be color blind, to choose my friends solely because their social interests coincided with mine – but no conscious black man can allow himself such luxuries in the contemporary world."

Walter Rodney
The Groundings with My Brothers

"It is not possible for human nature to change... If they had changed, we could not have found them bombing Afghanistan and Iraq."

Winnie Mandikizela-Mandela

"I am a Black man, An Afrikan man
Detained, But not destroyed
Enslaved, But not extinct
Conquered and Oppressed
But not for long.

I am a Black man, An Afrikan man
Fighting for the future/heading for home
Manhood, Be my momentum
Nationhood, Be my challenge
Familyhood, Be my reward."

George Edward Tait

"We do not want the word to get out that we wish to exterminate the Negro population and the Minister is the man who can straighten that idea out should the word get out to the more rebellious members of their population."

Margaret Sanger (1939) Eugenics and population control advocate

Foreword

Recent personal events have brought home (through the front door and into the living room) the frightening reality of the lives of our sons. In January 2006 my nephew was stabbed to death by a fellow 'Afrikan' son. His murder was the tragic consequence of a long-running feud between two groups of young Afrikan men, yet with one life gone and many more destroyed, none of those involved can say what the feud was about and how and why it started. Yet a young man, aged only 26 with his whole life ahead of him lies buried in the ground. His killer was in his early twenties.

Last year I gave birth to our first son. It is no under-estimation to say that my partner and I fear for him. We have absolutely no doubt that he will be raised in a loving environment (and, unlike many, he will have the 'privilege' of being raised in a two-parent household). But we know that that won't be enough to save him from the 'madness' taking hold in our communities. My nephew was raised in a loving household with a supportive family yet today two families still mourn his loss. The fact is we fear for our son so much we are seriously considering sending him to Afrika, because for all its supposed ills, it is the best place to ensure our son's mental, emotional and intellectual survival.

Our sons face a daily barrage of life-threatening challenges. It used to be the case that when you saw a fellow Afrikan in the street, you experienced a sense of security, a small moment, however fleeting, of belonging. We'd nod our heads at each other – an unspoken understanding – a common bond of colour and shared culture.

Ask many Afrikan boys now how they feel when they see another unfamiliar brother in their midst and the response can range from concern to palpable fear masquerading as macho bravado. Add to this mix the institutional racism in schools and the low expectation of Afrikan boys that make exclusion and prison seem like natural career progression; hip-hop artists who promote a value system of rampant consumerism without responsibility (it is literally the case of get rich and die trying); music that glorifies misogyny and the demeaning of women and a 'street' culture that emphasises "bling" over respect.

With the gun and the knife replacing debate and reason, broken family structure and poor family support systems replacing community, the future doesn't look bright; it certainly won't be orange and it definitely ain't gonna be Black. And if we are to save our sons – physically, emotionally and spiritually, we are going to have to employ strategies that effectively combat those ills that seek to destroy them.

"Saving Our Sons", adds considerable weight to the many books that provide us with those strategies. Brother Paul identifies and analyses the issues that face Afrikan boys in the UK (as well as US, Canada etc.) and provides recommendations and strategies (for parents and sons) to not only increase their chances of survival but to facilitate the nurturing of healthy boys (who can then develop into healthy men and contribute to the survival of the Afrikan race). It's not always easy reading for, as parents, we are forced to consider how we have contributed to the destruction of our children – both through action and omission.

Make no mistake, we as parents must take our share of the blame. Whilst we didn't create the cause, we certainly help perpetuate the effect. Boys look to us for guidance…in its absence they will look to each other, sometimes with disastrous consequences. We must recognise that the plight of our boys did not happen independently of us (parents/guardians and carers) but often because of us.

Question, when was the last time you looked at your child's C.D. collection? Do you monitor the pop culture that influences them? Has the TV, the internet and the iPod become your child's educator? Our failure to set and maintain value systems and principles; our failure to get involved in our children's education; our failure to talk to our sons and listen to their perspective on the issues that face them will be our failing of them. "Saving Our Sons" supplies the means and the mechanisms to literally save our sons and, if nothing else, supplies an opportunity to engage with them.

Our sons face a relentless battle for survival in this society but if we truly love them, we can help them win the war. See this book therefore as a powerful weapon in the process (no nuclear bomb 'ave nuttin pon dis!). Take the time to employ the recommendations – yes time is precious but giving up watching Coronation Street or EastEnders could not only help develop your relationship with your son but help him develop a better relationship with you, his environment, his community and start a process that could lead to a healthy and wholesome life.

It will be hard and there will be a lot of setbacks – but I would rather die than not try. Although my nephew has gone, he left behind him a wonderful legacy. Many of the lessons found in this book we will use with his brother and our son and whilst at times the battle may be lost the war for our sons has still to be won.

My partner wrote this poem a few years ago after another Afrikan son gave up on the gift of life.

Summer Fruit

How many Afrikan must tek dem life
Before we realise seh fruit musn't fall before dem ripe?

How many summers must we mourn?
For flowers that die, for seeds unborn.

How many roots must come to an end?
Before we understand seh a withered fruit
is the passing of another friend.

Is this really how the sons of Afrika must grow?
Is life what we reap and death what we sow?

How many times must a bredder die?
Before we realise seh dis is no harvest
But fruit – gone before dem ripe.

My partner and I are lucky; we share the same view of the world and take joint responsibility for the actions we need to take with our son. Together with our friends this may just be enough. For many mothers and fathers who have to make that journey on their own, –

some lucky enough to have great family and friends – we need to see family beyond biology. We need to remember that we are bound inextricably to each other despite whatever journey we have had to make. So when you see our son Ayodele on the street, remember this book – remember, that you too will help shape his destiny, because if you look into his eyes you'll see that he is your son too.

Nicola Grignon
(Poem by Robert Green)

CONTENTS

Introduction – Why the Need for this Book?

I was born in North London in 1966 and when I survey the so-called Black community in Nottingham where I now live, I am deeply worried. There are not many causes for optimism. When I survey the wider national UK scene there are still not many causes for optimism. When I look across the Ethiopian Sea (Atlantic Ocean) to the US, Brazil, Caribbean etc. I still do not see too many causes for optimism. When I look at Afrika I see even greater problems, but much greater causes for optimism. Why? Because the foundation for a people's liberation is the family and the family is still alive and kicking in Afrika despite rumours of its demise, whereas in the so-called 'West' the Afrikan family is facing meltdown.

Despite the title, this book is really about families and building up family life since we cannot save our sons without saving our families. This does not mean that this book offers a magical solution to reconstructing the Afrikan nuclear and extended family. No. This book is about working with what you have got and making the best of it. This book is not about blaming single parent households for all our ills, but neither is it about pretending that single parent households are a good idea. They are not. It is seriously hard for two parents to raise sane children in this cultural asylum, let alone one person and the nuclear family was never our cultural norm. The extended family is the Afrikan way. However we are where we are and we need to build from there.

When I was coming up I can never remember feeling fear at the sight of other young Afrikan males walking down the road. Nowadays our young men know that they are most likely to be seriously injured or murdered by someone who looks like them, sometimes for the most flimsy reason. I am not pretending that it was all sweetness and light back in the late '70's and early '80's, however most of my friends lived with their Mums and Dads who were married. All of our Dads were employed and all the Afrikan youth at my school stuck together. However some things have not changed. Most of my generation were still performing badly in school, went on to become over-represented in prisons, over-represented in mental institutions, went into unemployment or lower paid jobs and were confused about their Afrikan identity. So, some things change, but the overwhelmingly negative social and economic outcomes for Afrikans across the globe continues.

If you keep on doing the same thing you will always get the same result, therefore this book is about parents looking at how they communicate with and parent their teenage sons and teenage sons looking at how they communicate with their parents and the wider world. The aim is to raise up a generation of strong, productive, proud, young Afrikan-centred warriors who will commit themselves to the liberation of themselves and their people.

There have been other books written about raising Afrikan adolescents/young men to manhood. My hope is that this book can take its place amongst that literature and with its focus on parents and sons working through the book together to improve their relationship and clarify their roles, offer practical assistance to this current generation of parents and teenagers.

My credentials

I am not the father of a teenage Afrikan boy – my son will be ten in late 2006 – therefore I think it is important to set out why I think that I am capable of offering useful advice and insights to Afrikans who are the parents of teenage boys.

I have been working with Afrikan young men and boys since the early 1990's. My first experience of this type of work came when I was employed as an Employment/Training & Education Advisor by a charity working with prisoners and ex-offenders. Although the work was not specifically aimed at Afrikan prisoners, I used to run a pre-release course every two weeks at Glen Parva Young Offenders Institute which is one of the largest YOIs in Europe. This experience of working directly with young offenders (both inside and out of prison), a fair number of whom were Afrikan, gave me a good insight into the traps into which too many of our young men fall, which lead to the prison gates.

Since that time I have run a mentoring project for Afrikan and Dual Heritage young people at risk of school exclusion and/or

4

underachievement. In 1998 I and a colleague, Linda Wright, set up Nottingham Black Families in Education, a parent support group for the parents of Black children and I have acted as an educational advocate for the group for the past eight years, representing Afrikan young people (the vast majority of whom are boys) and their parents regarding issues of school exclusion, underachievement, school transfers etc.

I have organised an annual summer school, Kulture College, as part of an educational group, Nubian Link, for the past nine years. In 2003 I jointly organised and helped facilitate a programme for Black Young Offenders in partnership with the Nottinghamshire Youth Offending Team. I have been a founding member of an Afrikan men's group, Brother II Brother, since 1998 and have been through Rites of Passage training under the leadership of a twice initiated Yoruba Ifa priest Chief Alagba Olaitan (from Oyotunje Afrikan Village in North Carolina) and learned elder Baba Ademola. This training led to Brother II Brother developing our own rites of passage programme which was piloted with a group of young Afrikan men aged 17-23 and as I write these words this programme is being delivered with a group of Afrikan boys aged 10-12. I am also a founding member of the Afrikan Education Forum and have been fighting for the interests of Afrikan children and parents in education in Nottingham for a number of years.

This book has been inspired by, is dedicated to and comes out of a love for; our sons, who we can no longer continue to collectively fail.

There is a plague of anti-Afrikan propaganda in the media which is like an electromagnetic assault upon our senses and which is undermining our children's – and truth be told, ours as well – already fragile 'racial'/cultural identity. A people who fundamentally hate and are ashamed of who they are and where they come from cannot succeed in life and we are proof positive of that. Let's look at the contemporary manifestation of this self-hatred.

Niggeritis
We hear a lot about young Afrikans and increasingly Afrikan adults

referring to themselves and other Afrikans as 'Niggaz' (apparently this is the 'Black spelling!). I wrote about this in my first book, 'Niggers, Negroes, Black People and Afrikans' (2003), where I set out the psychology that underpins the use of these different terms and how this way of thinking shows itself in the way we behave.

I have come to the conclusion that the use of this type of self-hating language is a symptom of a syndrome, a mental illness that I define as 'Niggeritis'.

Definition – 'Niggeritis is a cultural virus; most commonly, but not exclusively, found amongst young Afrikan males, which presents itself via a range of anti-social, group and self-hating behaviours which the 'infected' comes to view as 'Being Black' or 'Keeping it Real'. This syndrome is also found in some older Afrikans (particularly males) and although on the surface the symptoms often appear less severe than in the young, it is in fact harder to treat older patients.'

The only known longlasting cure for Niggeritis is strong and regular doses of Afrikan-centred Love, Culture and Discipline leading to the formation of a positive Afrikan self concept.

Symptoms include:

- 'The Ghetto mumble' – Afrikan youngsters suddenly become incapable of speaking in clear, easily intelligible sentences, their vocabulary becomes highly restricted, with sentences built around words/phrases such as 'Like', 'Innit', 'Ya get meh' etc. and they speak with their head down and fail to make eye contact.
- Trousers in need of a waist – Young and not so young men walking around with most of their underwear exposed as if they are selling something!
- 'Yo my Nigga' – Use of the word 'Nigga' as some sort of term of endearment for other Afrikans. A belief that young people have 'reclaimed' the word Nigga.
- Use of violence as a means of communication – Violence becomes

6

a first resort for sufferers of this condition and it is viewed as normal to 'put yu gyal under manners'.

- Smoking weed (normally Skunk) and other narcotics as if it was going out of fashion – Get high in the morning, high in the afternoon and high in the evening.
- Lack of personal hygiene – Dem smell bad.
- Penis complex – Holds on to his dick as if he had lost it and just found it. Extreme preoccupation with sexual prowess and sexual activity.
- Rejects routines and disciplines
- Rejects learning as 'White'
- Preoccupied with obtaining flashy, expensive toys
- An almost complete lack of spiritual development (this does not mean religious belief)
- A deeply profound fear of failure (especially in relation to academic competition) – based upon a negative racial self-concept and lack of historical knowledge which leads them to believe that we have collectively never done anything, never will do anything, are intellectually inferior and therefore it is better not to try than to try and fail.

If you think about young people you know in your local community I am sure you can identify some who manifest a good number of these characteristics and many who display at least one or two.

Finally, if you want to see a graphic illustration of the war being waged on our sons take a look at the following graph which highlights the effect of White education on young Black minds in the absence of a strong protective culture.

The Facts and Figures

In 2003 Government, for the first time, produced statistics showing pass rates in GCSE's across ethnic groups. Black children start school as one of the highest achieving groups but leave school as the lowest achievers.

The chart below shows ethnic group performance compared to LEA average at each Key Stage

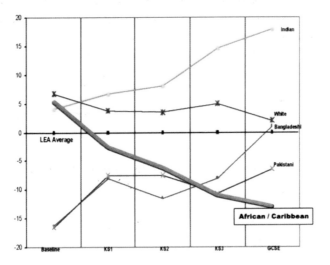

Source: National Black Boys Can Association leaflet

It is important to understand why other non-white groups are able to still achieve in a racist society whilst we continue to be intellectually disabled. The main factors are, firstly, we always get the most prolonged and brutal assault from White society since they have placed us at the bottom of the racial hierarchy that they invented. The nearer you are to 'Whiteness' the more acceptable you are. Secondly, no other group has been through the type of Maafa (sometimes labelled Black Holocaust) of enslavement and brutalisation that we went through and come out stripped of their language and culture. Culture is what protects these other groups against the effects of racism. Culture is what enables them to believe in themselves, trust, co-operate and work together and want to marry people who look like themselves. Most Afrikans in the 'West' and to some extent in Afrika have a neo-slave/neo-colonial (neo=new) culture that provides very little protection.

The solution is therefore simple (although horrific to most Afrikans in the 'West'), but difficult to implement. We have to re-Afrikanise ourselves. We have to do Sankofa, 'to go back and fetch that which has been left behind'. We need to follow the breadcrumbs back to the point where we were strong and powerful as a people. We need to adopt all the best parts of Afrikan culture, adapt them for our current situation and dash weh de slave business.

As Professor Wade Nobles says:

"If you have salt water fish in fresh water, what do you do? You put salt in the water."

Therefore if you have Afrikans adrift in a sea of European culture you have to put Afrikan culture in the water. Otherwise you get what he describes as 'strange behaviour'.

Hopefully you will find this book packed full of Afrikan sea salt.

N.B The terms Afrikan and Black are used interchangeably during the course of this book to refer to us. Terms such as Afrikan-Caribbean and Afrikan-American are used when I wish to refer to a specific Afrikan sub-group. As Mutabaruka says, No matter where you are born, if you are Black you are an Afrikan.

Who is this book aimed at?

Mums
You are always there when we need you, so I hope this book will be of assistance to you. Many of you will be raising a son without his father in the house. Whether this is your situation or not this book can help you in working productively with your son. However if you don't live with his father it should be particularly helpful. The teenage years (in fact from around age eight) should be father's/men's time to move centrestage in the raising of a boy into a man, however we all know that for a variety of reasons a lot of Dads are not able, or willing, to fully play their proper role in their children's lives. Therefore we will not dwell on what we can't change in the short-term, but rather what we can change and the easiest thing we can change is ourselves. We can change the way we think, speak and act and in so doing inspire and create change in others.

This book can be used to further cement and reinforce an already positive relationship with your son or as a chance to create a fresh start if things have not been going so well. I know a lot of Mums worry deeply about their sons when they see the culling of young Afrikan men in so-called Western societies. There are no guarantees in life for any of us, however the best protection we can provide for our sons is a knowledge of self, love of Afrikan people and a commitment to justice. Remember the Afrikan proverb:

'Once you conquer the enemy within the enemy without
can do you no harm'.

Dads
It is good to have you on board. As I suggested, in the foregoing section for Mums, this is your time. You need to show your son how to be a man and working through this book will be like holding up a mirror to your manhood. You will see yourself clearly, warts and all. It does not matter if there are more warts than face at present, what matters is that you commit from this point onwards to be the best man you can be. It is time for Black men to fix up and walk tall in the

world as men and not the pale imitation of Afrikan men that too many of us are. This book is going to lead your son to perhaps ask you some difficult questions and you know he is going to find your weak spot! Therefore my advice is to ask yourself these questions first!

'Discipline your sons until they can discipline themselves'

Sons
Wonderful son of Afrika, this book is for you and about you. A lot of the times it is going to feel that I am talking about you, sometimes talking at you and I hope some of the time communicating with you. I could have written a book just for you, however I need to get your parents on board, because in order for you to fulfil your potential your parents need to support you. This book is an encouragement and challenge to you. I am encouraging you to be the very best you can be and to succeed magnificently. I am challenging you to leave this 21st Century Nigga Culture behind and reject Black men acting like jesters, jokers, fools or thugs. Pull up your trousers, put on a belt, forget the ugly tattoos and read this book.

> "Thousands will tell you that it cannot be done, thousands will tell you that you will fail. But only you child will know how far you can sail. So say to yourself, 'I shall not fail.'"
> Marva N. Collins

You are our hope, joy and future and we Love you.

Grandparents, other adult relatives and significant adult others
You are supposed to be the support team, however sometimes you are in the front line as the Afrikan family continues to fall apart. You can use this book to support the boy(s) in question and importantly encourage his parents to take the actions that will help him to step up to the next level. You may need to have some open and frank conversations with the parent(s) since they need to take responsibility for driving this process and as I always say:

'Our children are not the problem, We are'.

Afrikan Activists working with Afrikan boys
Although this book is directed at Afrikan parents and sons it can be useful to people such as yourself delivering programmes for Afrikan male youth. Not only can the questions and recommendations be used to stimulate discussions with the youth you work with, you can show this book to parents and recommend that they use it with their sons.

This book is a challenge to Afrikan youth workers to stop feeding our youth Eurocentric cultural poison, to stop pandering to the belief that mediocrity, slackness, and stupidity are the hallmarks of Black culture and to start showing our youth the reality of the world we live in. Understand this. This book cannot be universalised for use with all youth or 'BME' youth. Whilst there may be some universal ideas contained within it (such as in the chapter on success) this book is written by an Afrikan for Afrikans, therefore it can only be used effectively in an all Afrikan environment.

The Eurocentric youth work paradigm has proven itself harmful to Afrikan youth, just as the Eurocentric social work paradigm has proven itself harmful to Afrikan families. If you are intellectually and emotionally locked into a European way of thinking and being you will not like this book. If you are seeking to become 'the Afrikan' there should be material to work with in this book.

Guidance for Parents as to How to Use this Book with your Son

The need for careful judgement regarding exposure
As discussed earlier, this book deals with some serious, critical issues in terms of the future prospects for Afrikan boys and young men. I have aimed this book at parents of teenagers and the teenage sons themselves. I have put together material that I believe is relevant to both groups, however it is your responsibility to check out this book and make sure you feel it is suitable for use with your son(s). **Be warned there is some fairly strong material in this book**, but nothing (in terms of the negative concepts discussed and depicted) that I believe your son will not already have been exposed to and this material is set in a context to uplift him and not to diminish him.

Please follow this guide as to how to use this book. Under no circumstances just give this book to your son and leave him to get on with it. Because I have described the nature of our oppression in clear terms this book could make a young person feel angry and if that happens that anger needs to be channelled towards constructive activity and purpose and not allowed to fester.

Read it first yourself
You should read this book from cover to cover yourself. I have deliberately made this book a lot shorter than my two previous books ('Niggers, Negroes, Black People and Afrikans' and 'Blue Skies for Afrikans') because I want you to read all of it. I am always amazed by people who say they buy books but never read them. This book is for reading and using. Make a mental note of the 'Questions for Afrikan Life' and Recommendations at the end of each chapter. You need to discuss these issues with your son.

Bringing your son into the picture
When you buy the book and bring it home, tell your son about the book and that you will be going through it with him. This should not be a request! He may not like the fact that you are saying that he has to read this book with you, however if you say he cannot read the

book until you have finished it you can almost guarantee that he will want to have a look inside!

One chapter at a time

Once you have prepped your son and read the book it is time to read together. Get your son to read to you as this will help you to assess his reading proficiency and comprehension skills. Whilst he is reading ask him questions about key points raised. Work out how many pages you want him to read before you start and the key questions to ask. Ideally get him to read 4-5 pages at a time and never more than one chapter in a day. If you are finding it hard to engage your son with the book let him choose the chapter that most interests him as the first chapter.

Questions and Recommendations

The questions and recommendations at the end of most chapters are crucial to getting the most out of this book. These questions need to be explored and discussed fully. Allow your son to express his opinions even if you do not agree with him. Ask him to evidence his opinions as this will aid critical thinking.

The recommendations are there to aid positive change. Look at these carefully with your son and identify those recommendations you are both willing to take on board. Circle these recommendations. You will use these in creating your Action Plan for change (see Appendix 1).

For things to Change we have to Change
(Example is Better than Precept)

'If you always do the same thing you will always get the same results.'

This book is asking you to engage in positive change, whatever your starting point, irrespective of whether you feel your son is in crisis or doing well. We can all do better and must all do better. Remember, 'Every day do your best and every day make your best better.' You may find that parts of this book make you feel uncomfortable. If that is the case please persevere. This book is not designed to make you feel comfortable, nor do I expect you to agree with everything I have written. This book is designed to challenge you and your son to be the best Afrikan parents and son you can be. We need to become the models for what we seek in our children.

A Time for Action

Once you have worked your way through the book, it is time to fill in the Action Plan. Go back through the recommendations at the end of each chapter and identify those you circled for action. These recommendations will become the tasks/objectives to be achieved in your action plan. Both you and your son need to complete an action plan. You can copy out the template and fill in the action plan. Once the action plan is completed make sure your son places it prominently on his bedroom wall and you do the same in your bedroom. Each of you needs to read your respective action plans daily for the first 30 days and then weekly until the action plan is fulfilled.

Congratulations

If you have completed all of the steps above you and your son are serious about his development. You are committed to positive change and to the upliftment of your people. Ashe Ashe Ashe (let it be so).

"There are Negroes who will never fight for freedom. There are Negroes who will seek profit for themselves from the struggle. There are even some Negroes who will cooperate with the oppressors. The hammer blows of discrimination, poverty and segregation must warp and corrupt some. No one can pretend that because a people may be oppressed, every individual member is virtuous and worthy."

Martin L. King, Jr.

The Crisis facing Black Young Men

We hear a lot of stuff about the progress Black people are supposed to be making in mainstream (which is code for 'White') society. The reality is that whilst some Afrikans are making a lot of money – which seems to be a lot of people's measure of success – the Black family has never been in such a mess as it is today and the future looked so grim for so many of our young men as it does today.

Please read the following reviews of academic reports in this chapter. There are statistics in this section; which immediately puts some people off, however these are important statistics which reinforce what we are witnessing with our own eyes, the destruction of our sons by a society which has no use for Afrikan men except as athletes, jesters and clowns.

If you want to know why there so many so-called absent fathers in our communities you need to go beyond stereotyping brothers as 'wotless dargs', lazy, no account, shiftless etc. etc. and understand that in general terms if you want to undermine a people's men and destroy the family unit, take away their jobs and economic prospects and make the Welfare State the Daddy. If these people have already been conquered by the dominant group in society – as we have – they will have developed a negative self-concept and unemployment and poverty will be the straws that breaks the Black Camel's back.

In an article entitled 'Plight Deepens for Black Men, Studies Warn' Baltimore journalist Erik Eckholm reviewed several academic studies which tell us what we should already know, namely that many Afrikan men are up s**t creek without an economic paddle.

Eckholm says that "Black men in the United States face a far more dire situation than is portrayed by common employment and education statistics...and it has worsened in recent years even as an economic boom and a welfare overhaul have brought gains to black women and other groups."

This should tell you that there is something special about the way Caucasians view the Afrikan man and something unique about the challenges that will face your son as he grows to manhood.

Eckholm goes on to suggest the "new studies, by experts at

Columbia, Princeton, Harvard and other institutions, show that the huge pool of poorly educated black men are becoming ever more disconnected from the mainstream society, and to a far greater degree than comparable white or Hispanic men."

This is a warning to all those 'BME edeats' (BME = Black & Minority Ethnic) in the UK and 'People of Colour fools' in the US who keep trying to lump Afrikan men in with all other non-White men and even non-indigenous White men (such as Eastern Europeans in the UK) and pretend that we all face the same problems. Let us be clear, we are on our own. These other non-White groups are our competitors, not our friends and allies.

"There's something very different happening with young black men, and it's something we can no longer ignore," said Ronald B. Mincy, professor of social work at Columbia University and editor of "Black Males Left Behind" (Urban Institute Press, 2006).

"Over the last two decades, the economy did great," Mr. Mincy said, "and low-skilled women, helped by public policy, latched onto it. But young black men were falling farther back."

Lesson – **Caucasian men would rather give a job to an Afrikan woman than an Afrikan man. Why? Men fear other men not women and also by helping more Afrikan women into employment and not helping Afrikan men, they keep our communities unbalanced and further undermine our families.**

Official unemployment rates can be misleading because they do not include those not seeking work or incarcerated.

There follows some of the main findings of these recent reports as set out by Erik Eckholm:

The share of young black men without jobs has climbed relentlessly, with only a slight pause during the economic peak of the late 1990's. In 2000, 65 percent of black male high school dropouts in their 20's were jobless – that is, unable to find work, not seeking it or incarcerated. By 2004, the share had grown to 72 percent, compared with 34 percent of white and 19 percent of Hispanic dropouts. Even when high school graduates were included, half of black men in their 20's were jobless in 2004, up from 46 percent in 2000.

Impact – No jobs, no money, no Daddy at home, but plenty of

Daddys in prisons.

Incarceration rates climbed in the 1990's and reached historic highs in the past few years. In 1995, 16 percent of black men in their 20's who did not attend college were in jail or prison; by 2004, 21 percent were incarcerated. By their mid-30's, 6 in 10 black men who had dropped out of school had spent time in prison. In the inner cities, more than half of all black men do not finish high school.

Explanation for our Sons – Prisons are the new plantations. Whilst they will let you sleep on the streets without a roof over your head, they will always find room to lock you up if you get involved in crime.

Listen to what two Afrikan men from a neighbourhood in Baltimore had to say. Curtis E. Brannon told how he quit school in 10th grade to sell drugs, fathered four children with three mothers, and spent several stretches in jail for drug possession, parole violations and other crimes.

"I was with the street life, but now I feel like I've got to get myself together," Mr. Brannon said recently in the row-house flat he shares with his girlfriend and four children. "You get tired of incarceration."

Mr. Brannon, 28, said he planned to look for work, perhaps as a mover, and he noted optimistically that he had not been locked up in six months.

"I don't understand," said William Baker, 47. "If a man wants to change, why won't society give him a chance to prove he's a changed person?" Mr. Baker has a lot of record to overcome, he admits, not least his recent 15-year stay in the state penitentiary for armed robbery.

Now out for 18 months, Mr. Baker is living in a home for recovering drug addicts. He is working a $10-an-hour warehouse job while he ponders how to make a living from his real passion, drawing and graphic arts.

"I don't want to be a criminal at 50," Mr. Baker said.

Lesson – There is nothing sadder than a man who realises he has wasted most of his life and his talents. You can never turn the clock back, you can only change the present and future.

According to census data, there are about five million black men ages 20 to 39 in the United States.

Caucasian academics, politicians and policy makers talk about terrible schools, absent parents, sometimes racism, the decline in manual jobs and a Black subculture that glorifies swagger and 'badness' over work as some of the various causes of the statistics set out above.

My interpretation – It is true that some Black men have learned to be irresponsible. Since slavery, until today, we have often been denied the opportunity to act like real men and yet have been criticised for not taking responsibility for our families and communities. Since we have not had control over our tomorrows, some of us have decided just to live for today and to hell with the consequences. Some of these brothers think to hell with the White man and his system, I will just do my own thing. They have treated us like boys, called us 'Boy' and too many of us have ended up acting like boys. This is not due to genetics or Black culture, it is a product of being conquered and oppressed. Therefore the only way for us to become whole men again is to overthrow our oppression.

We are at war but only one side is fighting. Jobs and prisons are just part of the battlefield. It is not nice but it is true.

Gary Orfield an education academic at Harvard University and editor of "Dropouts in America" (Harvard Education Press, 2004) says that "Closer studies reveal that in inner cities across the country, more than half of all black men still do not finish high school. We're pumping out boys with no honest alternative and of course their neighborhoods offer many other alternatives."

By 2004, 50 percent of black men in their 20's who lacked a college education were jobless, as were 72 percent of high school dropouts, according to data compiled by Bruce Western, a sociologist at Princeton and author of the forthcoming book "Punishment and Inequality in America" (Russell Sage Press). These are more than double the rates for white and Hispanic men.

One of the main factors that have reduced black employment in the US is imprisonment.

Lesson – They are locking Afrikan men up like there is no tomorrow. Men coming out of prison with criminal records aren't exactly prized by employers and studies have found that young Black men with clean records suffer by association. This is literally what they mean by the expression 'being tarred with the same brush'. If you are Black, you are Black, you are Black. And we all know (don't we?) what Black means in the collective White mind.

Bruce Western indicated that the crack epidemic (which the CIA and other government agencies kicked off) massively increased the number of brothers getting arrested and imprisoned in the US in the 1980's (and UK in the 1990's), but since then the political shift toward harsher punishments, more than any increases in criminal activity has accounted for the continued growth in the prison population.

Among black dropouts in their late 20's, more are in prison on a given day – 34 percent – than are working – 30 percent – according to an analysis of 2000 census data by Steven Raphael of the University of California, Berkeley.

Lesson about crime and punishment for our Sons – **They want your Black arse in prison and someone in prison may want your Black arse! Prisons are the new plantations used to warehouse 'useless' Afrikan men. They have a new term for the poor in the US – 'useless eaters'.**

In a society where higher education is vital to economic success, Mr. Mincy of Columbia University said that… "We spent $50 billion in efforts that produced the turnaround for poor women," Mr. Mincy said. "We are not even beginning to think about the men's problem on similar orders of magnitude."

Lesson – **Most Caucasians don't care, never have cared, never will care about Black men. It's up to us to climb out of the pit they have dug for us.**

Right, so we have seen a report from the US so lets move back across the pond to the UK so that I can show you that things are so similar in terms of the experiences of Afrikan men in the US and UK that it could not possibly be an accident. It's not, it is just the ideology of White Supremacy in action. Beware of Negro leaders like 'Uncle' Trevor Phillips who tell you differently. Be aware that the statistics and reports from the US are always more detailed, but that is only because they have more Afrikan men to destroy so they need to monitor progress more closely!

In an article by Christine Eke on the Colourful Network website 23/ 02/2006 the work of a leading criminologist Marianne Fitzgerald was highlighted.

"In the long term I had concerns about ways these figures might be interpreted as a measure of the scale of 'black criminality', even if this wasn't stated openly." commented Ms. Fitxgerald referring to the ethnic breakdown of crime statistics.

Ms Fitzgerald suggests that Black boys are victims of statistical racism and she believes that yearly crime figures only reinforce the negative stereotype of young black men as **'a problem'** to society.

Through extensive research Ms Fitzgerald, a Professor of Criminality at the University of Kent say she has found that street crime is unrelated to ethnicity but has everything to do with poverty and social circumstances.

Question – **Are poverty and social circumstances related to ethnicity.**

Answer – **For us Yes.**

Ms Fitzgerald who worked for the Home Office research unit for over 10 years was concerned about the way so called **'ethnic'** statistics were being used, particularly in the context of crime. She started by examining education statistics and then moved on to explore the notion of **'statistical racism'** through the publication of crime figures.

Her educational research led her to conclude that the education system (primary school to GCSE secondary stage) was letting down black children especially in poor areas.

Comment – **You don't have to be a Professor to work that out. This is called an academic statement of the bleeding obvious.**

"In discussion, I'd see kids who were unmistakeably bright but when I got them to fill in a short survey at the end of class, it was obvious they were being sent out into the world with a standard of

literacy which was lower than that of my 8 year old granddaughter even though they were nearly twice as old and just as bright. This meant their job prospects were poor; so their chances of legitimately earning the things they aspired to were very limited."

Ms Fitzgerald added: *"Yet, as I knew only too well, those in the poorest areas were surrounded by crime and opportunities for crime. Also very few of them were white but that was simply because these were areas that most whites had long-since abandoned."*

Comment – She fails to ask the most obvious question. Why do so many Afrikans live in poverty?

Statistical figures are used to monitor 'black criminality'

"The solution to statistical racism in the long-term, is to identify

all of the factors which produce these patterns in the figures and addressing the underlying causes – many of which have nothing at all to do with race and ethnicity." *Marianne Fitzgerald*

She has agreed with Trevor Phillips' admittance last year that black boys perform much worse in schools than white boys was true but pointed out that Asian boys from poor groups like the Pakistanis and Bangladeshis were also under-performing.

Comment – This is the old BME trick again to stop us focusing on ourselves. She does not mention that Afrikans outperform these groups and Caucasians at ages 5 and 7 but the longer our boys stay in school the worse they perform.

However when you contrast, pupils of Indian origin (a group on equal social-economic terms as whites) they actually do better than average, with Indian girls too out-performing whites in secondary schools.

The common denominator which stands out is ethnicity rather than race.

Comment – This is a case of Lies, White Lies and Damn White Statistics. White academics and Negro Leaders want to run away from 'race', even though that is how most of the latter group and

some of the former make their living from their White Masters. As I will show, in a later chapter on education, this issue has everything to do with 'race'. Bangladeshis have not been in the UK in significant numbers for as long as us but have gone past us in terms of educational attainment at school. Pakistanis are ahead of us as well and neither of these groups' men experience the same level of negative outcomes as Afrikan men. Indians should not even be brought into this discussion since Ms Fitzgerald, like all the other 'pseudu-liberal' academics, knows that far more of the Indians who came to the UK came from well-educated, middle class families and class is always a key factor in educational performance across all racial/ethnic groups.

Ms Eke reports that Ms Fitzgerald says that Trevor Phillips' suggestion that black boys be given separate treatment rings alarm bells about what has been referred to as 'statistical racism'. When analysing prison statistics she says she was labelled as a 'liberal' criminologist because she questioned the massive over-representation of black people but not 'Asians'.

Comment – Liberals and Negroes, a deadly combination. Note how she now lumps three Asian 'ethnic' groups, which are in fact nationalities, into one racial pot!

At the Home Office all major police forces were told that from 1996 they would have to provide annual statistics on stop/searches, caution and arrests broken down by ethnic group. To Fitzgerald it was obvious which group would come out on top.

She said: *"In the long term I had concerns about ways these figures might be interpreted as a measure of the scale of 'black criminality', even if this wasn't stated openly."*

She highlights there was *"a very pronounced degree of disproportion in the prison figures from the start."*

Similar patterns were also apparent in the Met's arrest figures *"which account for the bulk of any supposedly national statistics for black people anyway, because nearly two thirds of the total black population lives in London."*

"The immediate challenge is to stop the figures being read as if they told us some objective truth about essential differences between whole groups of people," she says.

Ms Fitzgerald suggests that "The solution to statistical racism in the long-term, is to identify all of the factors which produce these patterns in the figures and addressing the underlying causes – many of which have nothing at all to do with race and ethnicity. For example street crime as a result of poor housing, unemployment or even the pressure to have the latest designer labels."

Let's cut through this bull – Sadly Ms FitzGerald could not be more wrong. There is no such thing as 'statistical racism', there is racism as developed and practiced by the people who classify themselves as White and who created the idea of 'race' in the first place. She needs to ask herself why do Black people live disproportionately in the worst housing, have the highest levels of unemployment, go to the worst schools, get the worst treatment from mental health services, die disproportionately in police and prison custody, die younger, have more family breakdown, hate the way they look, marry out more than any other group etc. etc. etc.

Caucasian liberals – and no doubt their Negro followers will be on the case soon – are playing with 'statistical racism' and any new nonsense terms they can come up with while the Black house is burning down.

LEARNING FOR BLACK LIFE

Issues you and your son should discuss based upon the information contained within this chapter:

1. Why are there so many Afrikan men locked up in prison given our population?
2. Does your son think that prison is a reasonable place to be and if so does he understand what prison life is really like e.g. risk of physical and sexual assaults, loneliness, losing your girlfriend whilst locked up, emotional damage to children etc.?
3. Why are so many young Black men unemployed?
4. What does your son want to do for a living and is there a demand for this skill in society?
5. Does your son know how much money people generally earn from

this job or business?

6. Do you have a clear idea as to what grades your son expects to get at school? If not, you need to know and discuss.

7. Why do so many Black men live apart from their children and what effect does your son think this has on the men and their children, as well as, the mothers?

8. Do you know your sons friends and what do you know about their values and attitudes?

Welcome to Hell!

The Challenge of parenting in an anti-human, anti-Afrikan environment

Introduction

It is tough being a parent, especially in an alien, hostile cultural environment where your children are viewed as problems to be contained, detained, suppressed, repressed and if necessary terminated. We need to be unashamed to seek support from people who love and care about us. Parents often feel a sense of shame if their children are experiencing problems at school, particularly in relation to behaviour and exclusions. In small Black communities where too many people are preoccupied with 'free talk' and gossiping there is a sense that you don't wash your dirty linen in public. However it depends how you interpret the word 'public' and as I heard someone say 'if you don't air your dirty drawers they are going to stink'! On that basis we have some people walking around with some stink and crusty drawers on.

We have to face up to our parenting problems and seek out support if it is available. The extended family is the ideal place to start if there is stability present in your family network. If you live away from other family members or if they are not in a position to help, then friends and community organisations are the next port of call.

In terms of our boys the input of positive males is crucial. Even if the boy's father is active and positive it helps to expose your son to a range of positive males who can reinforce the home message and can sometimes mend bridges when there are difficulties at home.

Values as the foundation for Parenting and Living

At the end of the day we have to be clear about what will and will not make a difference to our sons. Not all of our boys will end up in high earning jobs even if they get a decent academic education and the financial payoff from education is a long way off, therefore the carrot of future high earnings is not enough to keep our boys on the straight

26

and narrow and away from the immediate rewards and allure of 'juggling'.

Materialism should never be the basis for seeking right conduct in our youth. Someone can always offer a quick illegal way to make money. We need to instil the right value system and not only reflect these values in all that we say and do, but help our sons to interpret and own these values.

Listed below are the **42 Declarations of Innocence** (*there are actually 147in total*) from Kemetic (ancient Egyptian) theosophy (spiritual philosophy). The ancient Kemites believed that when a person died they would enter a great Hall where their heart would be weighed on the scales of justice (this concept is Afrikan not European) against a feather. In order to proceed to the afterlife their heart had to be as light as the feather. In other words their heart had to be pure. As part of this process they had to be able to positively declare their innocence with regard to a whole range of negative behaviours. Unless the deceased could declare their innocence they would fail the test and their heart would be eaten by a pig (probably the origin of the taboo around eating pork in Judaism and Islam).

So you see, Afrikans in Kemet created a system of rules and codes to regulate human behaviour around four thousand five hundred years ago and it is from these Kemetic instructions that the Biblical Ten Commandments were derived around 1250 years later.

Action – Discuss these rules with your son and see what you think of them. Could they provide a basis for living today? How well do you both live up to these rules?

N.B. My interpretation of some of the rules is in brackets.

42 Declarations of Innocence
1. I have not done iniquity. (I have not committed a gross injustice)
2. I have not robbed with violence. (Street robbery etc.)
3. I have not done violence to any man.
4. I have not committed theft.
5. I have slain neither man nor woman. (Murder/manslaughter)
6. I have not made light the bushel. (Theft from employer)
7. I have not acted deceitfully. (Deception)

8. I have not purloined the things of the god. (Theft from temple or of offerings. Pastors please note!)
9. I have not uttered falsehood.
10. I have not carried off goods by force.
11. I have not uttered vile words. (Cussing, insulting people and carrying on bad)
12. I have not carried off food by force.
13. I have not acted deceitfully.
14. I have not lost my temper and become angry.
15. I have invaded no man's land. (White men please note)
16. I have not slaughtered animals which are the possessions of the Gods.
17. I have not laid waste to lands which have been ploughed. (Depriving people of the means to make a living)
18. I have not pried into matters to make mischief. (Gossiping and spreading rumours)
20. I have not given way to wrath without due cause.
21. I have not committed fornication, and I have not committed sodomy (Sexual promiscuity, sexual degeneracy, anal sex and other unnatural sexual acts)
22. I have not polluted myself. (Respect for your body)
23. I have not lain with the wife of a man. (Adultery)
24. I have not made any man to be afraid. (Intimidation)
25. I have not made my speech to burn with anger.
26. I have not made myself deaf unto the words of right and truth. (Defending something even when you know it is wrong)
27. I have not made another person to weep. (Cruelty)
28. I have not uttered blasphemies. (Respect for the divine)
29. I have not acted with violence.
30. I have not acted without due consideration. (Think before you act or speak)
31. I have not pierced my skin. (Look after your body)
32. I have not multiplied my speech beyond what should be said (Too much free talk is no good)
33. I have not committed fraud, and I have not looked upon evil.
34. I have never uttered curses against the king. (Respect legitimate

authority)

35. I have not fouled running water. (Protect the environment)
36. I have not exalted my speech. (Modesty in all things)
37. I have not uttered curses against God.
38. I have not behaved with insolence. (Manners maketh man [and woman])
39. I have not been guilty of favoritism. (Treat people on their merits)
40. I have not increased my wealth except by means of such things as are mine own possessions. (Don't exploit people to gain wealth)
41. I have not uttered curses against that which belongeth to God and is with me.
42. I have not thought scorn of the god of the city.

Some of these declarations are related and seem repetitious, however it just goes to show how seriously our ancestors took right conduct.

For those of you who have absorbed European lies about Kemet just take a look at the brother in the picture below. His name was Narmer or Aha (misnamed Menes by the Greeks) and he reunited upper and Lower Kemet and was the first Pharoah. Have you ever seen a European, Arab or other Asian with features like him? Maybe your son could get his history teacher to put up his picture in school and include him in any teachings about the ancient Egyptians.

Let's move on now and look at some day to day tips on parenting.

Recommendations for Parents

The following recommendations are taken from a brief paper produced by Paul Obinna Wilson-Eme, one of the leading Afrikan-centred thinkers in the UK. Paul is a qualified teacher who taught in Mosside, Manchester for more than a decade and has also taught in South London. Working alongside his friend, Lance Lewis, Paul was the creative force behind the highly acclaimed 'Education of The Black Child' conferences held in Manchester which were attended by some of the leading Afrocentric scholars in the world. Paul has been working with our children, young adults and older adults for many years and can just as accurately be described as a scholarly activist as an activist scholar.

Media
1. Gain more understanding of media influences.
2. Lower the 'volume' in the home. (i.e. one media source at a time!)
3. Let children see <u>you</u> reading and doing things with them you expect them to do.
4. Watch and listen to the media <u>with</u> them and discuss the content so that they form opinions along with you (reasoning/argument).
5. Be aware of 'Soap Opera' problem solving and 'Chat Show' social manners from yourself and them.
6. Put a cover on the television so that there has to be a positive action before switching it on.

Language
1. Invest in an extensive dictionary (with Etymology).
2. Build up your own understanding of words and use them wisely and in context (vocabulary or <u>Nommo</u>).
3. Correct yourself if you make an error in front of your children.
4. Apologise if you drop a 'cuss'.
5. Listen out and correct Grammar to help your children select the correct language code for the context.

Culture

1. Balance the discipline holistically. Remember 'the wor
2. Stop the use of 'nothing' as a denial word.
3. Encourage the leaving of the bad spirit at the door! "Lef i street"!
4. Immediately correct negative Non Verbal Communication. i.e. 'Cut Eye' and 'Kissing Teeth' and be aware if this is what you do.
5. Do not treat the child as though they are 'size' to lessen your responsibility to them. Show and build the '3 R's' in them (Reasoning, Respect and Responsibility).

General

Seek to understand and teach the wisdoms of the 2 P's (Proverbs and Parables).

Read the works of Amos Wilson, Jawanza Kunjufu, Paul Hill Jr., Na'im Akbar, Mary C. Lewis and Nathan and Julia Hare and apply the theories.

One of the issues Paul Obinna Wilson-Eme often talks about during his workshops/seminars is emotional literacy and that great ancestor Amos Wilson (1987) set out systematically how powerfully negative emotions such as frustration – which he saw as endemic to the 'Black Condition' in the US and Afrikan world – can affect an Afrikan's ability to parent effectively. I have partially reproduced a table setting out these effects below:

Parental Frustration Symptoms	Parental Attitudes and Childrearing Practices
Powerlessness	Lack of interest in maintaining control over child, feels powerless to effectively control child's destiny,...
Inability to Delay Gratification	Tends to act with hostility towards child when it is perceived as a hindrance to parental pleasure,...

Apathy	Fails to take deep interest in child's development, neglect of child's mental, physical and emotional wellbeing,...
Denial of Worthiness of Social Goals	Not interested in being a socially acceptable model for child to imitate,...
Fatalism	Believes the child's growth and development is a matter of luck, believes that deliberate efforts in child-rearing are futile,...
Low Achievement Motivation	Not highly motivated to achieve optimal circumstances for self development and the child's development, does not motivate the child to achieve,...
Ego-restrictiveness	Parental self is the main source of interest, the child is secondary, the home is not child-centred, takes little interest in the child as an individual,...
High Interest in Diversive Activities	Interested mainly in "pastime" activities, not problem-solving activities, which leads to child neglect, only interested in playing with or distracting the child as a means of dealing with its problems,...
Unrealistic Striving	Parental unrealistic striving alienates self and child, leaves inadequate time for proper child-rearing, teaches child to pursue goals beyond its inherent, acquired, and attainable talents, powers and means,....

Table 6

Source: The Developmental Psychology of the Black Child Amos N. Wilson (1987) pgs 57-59

Conclusion

Discuss your values with your son, where they come from and what they mean to you. Ask him about his values, where they come from and what they mean to him. Use values not bribery or coercion (threats) as the basis for your parenting and follow the tips in this chapter. Finally, don't wait for the house to burn down before you ask for help!

Key Issues

ⅈ it mean to be a Man? – Cross-cultural notions of manhood

Aʃʞ your son these two simple questions:

Q. What is it to be a man?

Q. When will you know that you are a man?

In fact, maybe you should ask and answer these questions for yourself before you move on to your son. These are absolutely crucial questions that we as parents need to be clear about. Forget liberal notions about life as a journey of self-discovery, our children need signposts to guide them on their way.

Let me set out for you some ideas about manhood that you can consider and share with your son once he has answered these two questions.

One of our greatest thinkers, Amos Wilson, tells us:

"....all societies distinguish between male and female; all societies also provide institutionalized sex appropriate roles for adult men and women." (Wilson 1991: 42)

Listed below are some of the ways Afrikan men are portrayed and the roles they are given in Caucasian societies.

Pimp
Wifebeater
Drug dealer
Rapist and Sexually Obsessed
Lazy
Violent
Physically Strong
Intellectually Weak
Absent Father

Smell bad
Mentally Ill (Crazy)
Entertainer
Athlete
Prisoner

Q. Parent – How do you see Black men? (be completely honest)

Let us now look at what most societies expect of men. Amos Wilson, who we quoted above, suggests that there some important issues in thinking about what makes a 'real man':

- The idea of manhood helps to bind men into society and to help make males productive,
- The idea of being a man is created by the group out of its culture and is not just about how the individual 'feels',
- Real manhood is not just about anatomy e.g. hair around your balls, it is something that must be proven i.e. you must be tested and overcome this test,
- The more difficult and harsh the environment the more the idea of manhood is stressed as a source of inspiration,
- Physical courage in defence of the group is found as a criteria across nearly all cultures,
- Real men give more than they receive,

So we can see that being an Afrikan man and being an Afrikan adult male are different. The only thing they have in common are the physical signs of adult male development e.g. deeper voice, body hair, facial hair, physical strength, the ability to produce children.

Let us be clear that White men are happy to see Black males acting like boys in men's bodies. White men do not want to see real Black men who love their people and are willing to stand up and fight for freedom, however this is exactly what you will have to teach (and allow) your son to do if you want him to be a *real man*.

So, I am suggesting that Afrikan men should show the following behaviours/qualities in order to maximise their potential:

- Loves Afrikan people
- Has a spiritual life that reinforces Afrikan culture and identity
- Never abusive to women
- Only uses violence in self-defence or defence of others
- Loves children
- Marries an Afrikan woman
- Takes pride in self without being vain
- Reads regularly
- Does not get high with legal or illegal drugs
- Loves to learn and develop their intellect
- Takes moderate exercise
- Learns how to manage money
- Never becomes a slave to a job
- Respects elders
- Remembers his ancestors by calling their names (libation)
- Moves with positive people
- Shows integrity, honesty and unselfishness in all he does

LESSONS FOR AFRIKAN LIFE
Questions to be discussed based upon the information in this chapter:

1. What makes a good Black man?
2. Name all the Afrikan men you know locally whom you admire and identify their positive qualities,
3. If your son's father does not have regular contact with him discuss with him how he feels about this situation,
4. Name all the Afrikan men from history whom you admire and identify their positive qualities,
5. Discuss how Afrikan men are portrayed in the media. Look at films, music videos and news stories on TV and in newspapers. Do a review of one day's television coverage. Is it positive or negative?
6. Many of our great leaders have been killed and/or attacked by Caucasians e.g. Marcus Garvey, Malcolm X, Steve Biko. Discuss this with your son. Does he think this makes Black men afraid to stand up for our people? How does it make you and him feel about

him fighting for our people?

Recommended Reading:

Black Men: Obsolete, Single, Dangerous? – Haki Madhubuti
Asafo: A Warrior's Guide to Manhood – Mwalimu K Bomani Baruti

How schooling puts Black boys off Learning

Q. What is the purpose of education? – Parent and Son to discuss

In the UK the education system was traditionally designed to meet the needs and develop the potential of around 10% of the population. These people were overwhelmingly males from the upper and middle classes and were the people who were chosen –mainly through birth – to rule British society or to manage companies and institutions on behalf of the ruling class. The 'education' given to the White working class was designed to teach them to know their place and to be ready to work hard in factories.

By the time I went on to Higher Education in 1984 still only around 15% of my age group were going on to Higher Education and it is only in the last 10 years that we have seen the huge increase in the proportion of young people going into Higher Education.

Q. If the education system was not designed for the White working class why do you think the rulers of this society will be concerned about educating Afrikan children?

Education is always about teaching *social conformity* i.e. it teaches children how to fit into the norms and values of the wider society. If the society is Racist it will teach children to accept the racial caste system. That means it will reinforce the idea of White over Black.

Q. What should an Afrikan-centred education teach our children?

Education should enable our children to answer the following questions:

1. Who am I? (As an Individual and as part of a community)
2. Where am I going? (Mission and Purpose in life)
3. What do I need to get there? (Skills, Experience and Knowledge required)
4. What are my responsibilities (To self, family, community,

ancestors, Creator)
5. How do I understand/see the world and what do I believe in? (Culture and Values)

Q. Ask yourself and then your son the five questions above. Most adults, let alone children, will struggle to answer all five with confidence. If this is the case it tells you that you have not been fully educated.

Two Afrikan scholars from the US, Nathan and Julia Hare, suggest that education consists of three main areas of activity or learning:

- **Cognitive** (basically the development of thinking skills and the ability to order and process information)
- **Affective** (knowledge of self, development of moral/ethical ideas and emotional intelligence)
- **Functional or Socio-Cultural** (Knowledge of how the society you live in really works. What are the written and unwritten rules. The ability to use cognitive and affective knowledge for the benefit of self, community and society).

Most schools are not effectively teaching our children cognitive skills. When they teach affective knowledge it is anti-Afrikan and reinforces European values and identity. Few schools attended by Afrikan children develop socio-cultural knowledge in our children. For example how many schools teach financial literacy? The answer is hardly any.

"One of the most tragic beliefs widely shared by Blacks throughout the world is that White-controlled educational institutions – regardless of whether they are elementary schools or universities – will educate our children. Faith continues to prevail in spite of overwhelming evidence which disputes this belief. Blacks continue to ignore the irrefutable truth that, in a racist social system, all institutions will reflect, protect, and sustain values that are consistent with racism. This should not be considered surprising or profound since all institutions serve to perpetuate the social theory of the group which created them. Therefore in any social system established by Whites, the institutions will reflect racism." (Wright 1984: 31)

This is the genius that was Bobby Wright describing institutional racism in a far more profound and meaningful way than Lord Macpherson (author of the Stephen Lawrence enquiry report) or any of his Caucasian legal predecessors ever have or could.

It seems to me that there still remains, a nagging, unspoken question mark – in the very deepest parts of the average Afrikan's mind – as to the intellectual capability of Afrikan people. That is to say, just as Afrikans proclaimed 'We are Black and We are Proud' as an antidote to our feelings of lack of racial self-worth, just as we proclaimed 'My nose is broad, my hair is curly, my lips are thick, my skin is black and I am beautiful' as an antidote to the reality of the self-hatred many Afrikans felt about the way they looked, so we talk about our genius stemming from the genes-in-us as a defence against the internalisation of racist stereotypes that place us at the bottom of a Caucasian conceived human intellectual ladder.

Q. Do you and your son really believe that we are as intelligent as any other group of people? If so why do we continue to 'underachieve'? Discuss.

Q. How are Afrikan Children doing at School?

The MisEducation of Afrikan Children in Nottingham – A Case Study

The following information is taken from a report produced in Nottingham looking at educational achievement.

EDUCATIONAL ATTAINMENT – FOCUS ON BLACK BOYS

How Are Black Boys Performing

Nottingham reflects the national picture of negative outcomes for Black boy pupils by the time they reach Key Stage 4 (GCSEs). The most recent national GCSE figures confirm this fact, with 37.5% of Black Caribbean pupils and 43.3% of Black African pupils achieving 5 or more GCSEs with C grades or better, compared to the national average of 52.3%. In Nottingham the figures for the most recent year, 2004, are as follows:

Ethnic Description	Number of Pupils	% Achieving 5+ A*-C
Caribbean	61	23
White And Black Caribbean	39	12.8
Other Black Background	39	15.4
African	11	45.5
White and Black African	10	20
City Total – All Ethnic Backgrounds Male Pupils	1368	35.2

Table 1 – Key Stage 4 achievement by Ethnicity

The table above shows that only one group of Black boys, those of African background, achieved a score higher than the city average and none of the groups achieved a score comparable to the national average. This low level of achievement was not reflected in the scores of boys from other ethnic minority backgrounds. For example, boys

43

from Indian backgrounds scored 70%, those from Bangladeshi backgrounds 66.7% and those from Pakistani Backgrounds 53.9%.

Lesson – Forget the BME/People of Colour Crap. Our boys are failing badly. You should note that 'Africans' in Nottingham do better than 'other Black groups' because they have not been culturally assimilated yet and have stronger a family structure i.e. more stable families with Dads living with their children.

Performance Across the Range of Key Stages

Of importance to note is that the performance of Black Caribbean and Black Other pupils at the first monitored key stage is higher than for all other ethnic groups (***This reinforces the point made by Amos Wilson in his book 'The Developmental Psychology of the Black Child' [1987] regarding the precocity (outstanding talent) of Afrikan children.*** The decline in performance over the school career of these pupils is therefore more severe than for any other group of pupils. The graph below illustrates attainment of Nottingham pupils compared to the national average in 2003 across all key stages.

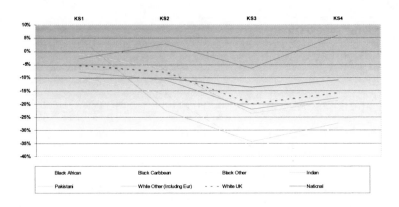

Graph 1 – Difference in attainment of Ethnic groups in Nottingham, compared to the National Average – 2003

The importance of this graph, in a Nottingham context, is that this is the first cohort that has gone through the whole of their secondary schooling under the management of Nottingham City LEA and for whom progress can be tracked and trends analysed. In future years it will be possible to track performance of pupils as individuals and groups and trends for gender and ethnicity will be far more apparent.

Explanation – The real importance of this graph is that it highlights that despite experiencing disproportionate poverty, single parent households, poor housing and living environments Afrikan/Dual heritage children come to school equipped to learn. It is the education system that is underachieving not Afrikan/Dual Heritage children.

As can be seen all groups of pupils suffer a drop in performance between Key Stages 1 and 3, with a rally in performance for Key Stage 4. It is commonly acknowledged that the transition period between leaving primary school and the first couple of years of secondary schooling (Key Stages 2 –3) is marked by a decline in relative academic performance for all pupils. The inference that could be drawn from the very marked decline in the performance of some black pupils between Key Stages 1 and 2, is however, that the problems that result in overall poor performance of black boys in GCSE results are already manifest between the ages of 7 and 11. It would therefore suggest that early interventions (i.e. at the upper primary level – age 7+) are necessary to sustain the educational performance of black boys. The scale of the issue is significant as Nottingham has the largest Black primary population outside of London.

Lesson – The problems start from the first day our children enter the school gates and are already noticeable by the time many of our boys reach age 7. Primary schools soften them up and Secondary school helps to finish them off.

Exclusions
Whilst the levels of permanent exclusions are reducing (1.7 per 1000 this year compared to 2.3 per 1000 last year), Black pupils in Nottingham have experienced disproportionately high levels of permanent exclusions from 2001 to 2004 from Nottingham City

schools. (See graph below). There are also significant levels of exclusion of City resident pupils from County schools, also disproportionately affecting Black pupils.

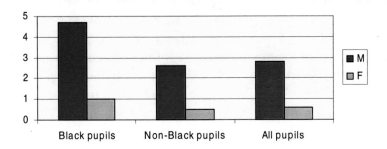

Graph 2 – Permanent Exclusions (rate per 1000) from 2001-2004 *(Nottingham)*

Lesson – **School exclusion can be like a passport to prison. If we have decided to put our children in White schools we must keep them in school until we have a better alternative.**

Conclusions

The vast majority of Caucasian educationalists, cling grimly to the 'conventional' (in other words Eurocentric) explanation with regard to the 'underachievement' of Black children.

This 'White mind' places the blame squarely at the feet of our children themselves, their feckless single parents (that's some of you), the wider Black community (that's all of us) and lastly, but by no means least 'Black street culture'. In this world it is the anti-intellectual, anti-learning cultural environment that Black children are raised in that is the cause of the problem and against which brave and heroic Caucasian teachers are forced to battle every day.

As with every good lie there is a germ of truth within the foregoing explanation. The truth is that the Black family **is** in crisis. The truth is that children raised in single parent households are more likely to live in poverty. The truth is that you will find many Black children who say they dislike or even hate school – although this is very different to hating learning.

The truth is that there is a sordid, grimy, anti-social Black sub-culture that is promoted by Caucasian owned record, film, radio and Television companies and presented as if it is the embodiment of 'Black Culture'. Some of our sons are being seduced by the idea of 'Street Life' and 'Ghetto Fabulous'. I know of Afrikan youth from very stable, loving homes who have decided to go 'juggling' on the street and have ended up in disaster. We have a responsibility to give our sons boundaries, focus and a race conscious identity that will mean that they would never prey on and victimise their own people.

LESSONS FOR AFRIKAN LIFE

Here are some points you can discuss based upon the information contained in this chapter:

1. Do you think there is any evidence that Black children enter school with a negative attitude to education?
2. Why were Black children performing so badly – and being classified as ESN (Educationally Sub-Normal), as opposed to the current SEN (Special Education Needs) – in the UK education system between the late 1940's and early 1980's even when most were living in stable two parent households, when our music still had a high proportion of consciousness, and our parents came from a culture in which education was highly prized?
3. Given all of the trials and tribulations of Black people, how do you explain the fact that Black children outperform all other groups at key Stage 1 (not just in Nottingham but in many other cities in the UK)? If our parents are not interested in education, if our children are more likely to live in poverty and if they are nurtured in a negative Black culture, how on Earth do they achieve this miracle? Are they genetically superior?
4. How is your son doing at school? Do you both know how he is doing in comparison to his classmates, the city average, and national average?
5. Most high paying jobs increasingly require knowledge of science and technology. How is your son doing at Maths?
6. Is your son as confident in the classroom as on the sports field?

7. What does your son want to do as a career? Have you discussed this and what is required to enter these professions?
8. Have you discussed your son eventually setting up his own business?

Recommendations

For parents:

1. Make sure you know what homework your child gets and establish a homework timetable. Put homework before recreation when your son gets home from school.
2. Agree realistic but stretching academic targets with your child.
3. Reward hard work and achievement. It does not always have to be financial.
4. Always put Academics before Athletics.
5. Ensure your child has a bedtime even if think they are too big. If they are at school they are not too big.
6. Encourage your child to form study circles with their peers at school.
7. Always attend parents' evenings.
8. If you have serious complaints about your child's treatment at school put it in writing.
9. View your child's school file at least once a year. It is your right.
10. Send your child to Saturday/Supplementary school if there is one in the area. Exposure to positive all Afrikan environments will be good for them.
11. Teach your son that the primary purpose of school is not to meet friends, check gyal etc. but to develop the knowledge, skills and understanding to allow them to look after themselves and their community in the future.
12. Expose your child to non-stereotypical career options.
13. If you don't know your own history you can't teach your child. If you don't teach your child their history someone else may teach them a warped version.

For sons:

1. Don't believe that you can get away with what your White peers get away with.
2. Don't confuse not liking your History teacher with not liking History. The same goes for all other subjects.
3. Your teachers get paid whether you succeed or fail and some of them don't care whether you succeed or fail. When you start ramping at school you are hurting yourself not them.
4. Approach academics the same way you approach sports, rapping, dancing etc.
5. It is not being Black to be stupid.
6. You need to work twice as hard as your White peers to get the same results in life.
7. Remember – Success is your Birthright! Go for it.

Recommended Reading:

The MisEducation of the Negro – Carter G. Woodson
The Hare Plan – Nathan and Julia Hare
Lateral Thinking – Edward De Bono
Countering The Conspiracy to Destroy Black Boys Vols I-IV – Jawanza Kunjufu
Motivating and Preparing Black Youth to Succeed – Jawanza Kunjufu
The Psychopathic Racial Personality and other Essays – Bobby E Wright
Blue Skies for Afrikans – Paul Ifayomi Grant

Money – A Substitute for Black Power

"Power is the ability to cause or prevent change."
Rollo May (Power and Innocence, New York: Norton 1977)

"Power is the Ability to define Reality and have other people respond to your definition as if it were their own."
Wade Nobles

Afrikan people need Power. In order to get power we need to understand what it is. The two definitions above are a good starting point. Power is about making things happen or stopping them from happening. Power is also about controlling the way people see the world.

Crucial Understanding – **Afrikan men have been conquered worldwide by Caucasian men, therefore Afrikan people have been conquered by Caucasian people.**

This may be a bitter pill for Afrikan men and boys to swallow, however swallow it we must. Why do I frame this statement in terms of men? Am I being sexist?

No. Put quite simply, we live in a patriarchal (male dominated) world. In every country on Earth men are in a generally dominant position over women, regardless of whether there are women in high status jobs or elected to high office. Men generally have more muscle mass and are more aggressive than women. The world is out of balance. Europeans have always been fearful of their women and suppressed them (e.g. Persecution and murder of millions of women as witches in Europe in the Middle Ages). Afrikan men are not and have never been perfect, but we did once do a lot better than we are now doing in terms of how we treat sisters. Afrikan women in many parts of the continent, be it the Igbo women in what is now Nigeria, the Ashanti women in what is now Ghana, or as far back as the women of ancient Kemet (Egypt), had real power and created and maintained social institutions e.g. women's societies to ensure fair and balanced relations between women and men.

As we lost our culture and took on other people's patriarchal religions so that changed.

Therefore to get back to the original point, **in a world dominated by men; Black men will have to take back power from White men – and any other group of men who wish to oppress us – and only then will it be possible for both Afrikan men and women to be free.**

Learn this, the meek shall inherit the Earth when the strong decide they are tired of having Power, which will be never. Or, put another way:

"The most dangerous of all dependencies is to depend on your powerful oppressor to free you and share power with you, because powerful people never train powerless people to take their power away from them."
John Henrik Clarke

Afrikan people will never be respected until there is a powerful Afrikan country that can stand toe to toe, eyeball to eyeball with the most powerful Caucasian and Asian countries and demand and enforce justice. It does not matter how clever you are as an individual, how much money you have, how nice you are, how handsome you are, you will still be part of a disrespected race. As Malcolm X said:

"What is a Negro with a PhD? Answer, Still a Negro."

For Sons – Your individual achievement only makes sense if it is helping to uplift Afrikan people.

We need to change the way we think, speak and act. I still hear Afrikan men referring to Caucasian men collectively as *'The Man'*. Well, if Caucasians are the men what are we? Logic dictates that we must be either Women, Girls, Boys or Babies. This perhaps explains why increasing numbers of Afrikan men are acting like pseudo-women and also why Caucasian men have historically (since they conquered and enslaved us) referred to Afrikan men as *'Boy'*.

Many Afrikan people pretend that Black people in 'big jobs' given to them by Caucasians = Black Power. This is neo (new) slave thinking. Kofi Annan (Head of the United Nations) has no independent power (but a Blonde wife of course). Condeleeza Rice (US Secretary of State for Foreign Affairs), who we are told is the most powerful woman in the world, has no independent power. They were both given their positions by Caucasian men, they both report to Caucasian men and they are both **willing** instruments of White Power.

Many Afrikans in 'the West' are little more than neo-slaves in suits working on bureaucratic plantations. If you want to know how much independent power we have; count the number of Afrikans you know who can and will speak out openly against White Supremacy. Very few, I think you will find. This is because we are nearly all employed by White people and we know that if we do anything to attack their system of White Power they will attack us and one of the best ways to do that is to take away someone's job. 68-70% of Afrikans in the US work for some branch of the government and over 50% of Afrikan graduates in the US work for the government. Only 2% of Afrikans in the US work for or own a Black business. The situation is very similar in the UK. This is a dangerous dependency.

Remember the saying:

'Don't bite the (White) hand that feeds you.'

Black Power requires Black people to organise as Black People first and everything else second, as Walter Rodney indicated in the quote at the beginning of this book. Marcus Garvey called this 'Race First'. Oh, and don't let any Negroes or White liberals tell you that this is racism in reverse. This is what all other people on Earth who have sense do. They use their race/ethnicity/culture as the basis for pooling their resources and gaining power. Claude Anderson in his book 'Powernomics' calls this *'ethno-aggregation'* (Anderson 2001).

The Colour of Money
Money is not power, it is a tool used by people with power and loaned to people without power. Money is not real, it is a system created to simplify the exchange of goods and services i.e. it was easier to buy and sell goods using money than to exchange goods and

services by bartering. When you give someone money you are making a promise that if they give someone else that note they can get some goods or services in exchange for it. That is why notes are called 'promisary notes'.

On a global level people who control the value of money (currency exchange rates) control economies. At the moment it is mainly Caucasian men working for Caucasian institutions who carry out this role. On a local level people who freely give their money to other groups of people will suffer and be poor. This is what Afrikans do more than any other people, hence we are poor.

Note – **Think Black, Buy Black, to get us Black on Track**

Bling, Ice and dem kinda ting

Why do so many Afrikans waste so much money on expensive crap, trying to look as if we have money when comparatively few of us have any real wealth?

Anyone can buy a thick gold chain dug out of the earth by poor Afrikans on the motherland who are exploited by White owned corporations.

Anyone can buy diamond encrusted chops dug out of the earth in war-torn Afrikan countries by poor Afrikans exploited by White corporations. They call these conflict-gems and most diamonds are conflict-gems.

White marketing experts call this behaviour 'conspicuous consumerism'. The tendency of some people to buy highly visible (conspicuous) goods. Target Marketing, a US based company providing marketing information for corporations around the world, have noted the tendency of Afrikans in the US to spend money far in excess of their population, income or wealth on items such as Cars, Wide Screen/Plasma TVs, MP3 Players, DVDs, mobile phones, jewellery, alcohol, cigarettes, Cinema tickets. That is to say we spend a greater proportion of our money on consumable (things you use once such as alcohol and cigarettes) and depreciating (things that lose value such as cars) items than all other people in the US, even though we are one of the poorest groups in the US.

Just so you know, Afrikans in the US:

- Are **12%** of the population
- Earn **7%** of the total US income
- Own less than **3%** of the wealth in the US
- But provide more than **30%** of cigarette, alcohol, cosmetics, cinema and Cadillac sales

The last bullet point above represents the behaviour of a conquered people trying to forget the fact that they are oppressed and depressed; by consuming legal (and illegal) drugs or buying expensive toys.

Unfortunately it is more difficult to get this type of data for Afrikans in the UK, however I can guarantee you that the patterns of expenditure are very similar.

What is Wealth?
Many people in general, and many Afrikans in particular, are confused about the difference between *Income* and *Wealth*.

Income is the money you have coming into your household each week or month. This could come from a salary, pension, interest from savings, dividends from shares, benefits/welfare, rental income from another house you own etc.

Wealth is the total value of all your assets minus the total value of all your debts or liabilities.

Assets include the value of your house, car, furniture, jewellery, stocks and shares, cash, savings etc.

Liabilities include your mortgage, overdraft, credit card debts, loans, hire purchase etc.

Most Afrikans, even in rich countries such as the US and UK, have very little wealth even though they may have quite high incomes. We produce very little, but are the greatest consumers in the world which is why any new immigrant group arriving in the US or UK heads straight for the 'Black areas' to set up their shops.

Son – **Your task as an adult will be to work with other Afrikans to create wealth for yourself and our people. This wealth must be created without hurting other people or the environment.**

Power to Some of the People

Sons – Let us look at some of the people with power that you will have to deal with in your life:

Parents – Your parents are a source of *legitimate authority* in your life. They are your guardians and have a responsibility to guide you responsibly through childhood and onto an independent adulthood. You will never be *size* with them even if you live to be 100 years of age. Your job is to listen, obey and question respectfully so that you can learn the lessons of life. Unfortunately, too many parents and too many sons have forgotten their roles and we have adults dressing and acting like teenagers and teenagers taking on adult behaviours without responsibility. Children should not have adult rights because children should not have adult responsibilities. For example children get shorter sentences for criminal behaviour because of their age and in the UK if a child is aged below 10 they cannot be held criminally responsible. This is not the same as saying that children should not be protected or respected. If you want to get more information on Parenting see my book '*Blue Skies for Afrikans*' (Grant 2005).

Teachers – Are supposed to carry out their role in accord with the principle '*loco parentis*' which literally means local parent. Now you may well be thinking that your teachers don't act like your parents and that you don't want them to. Well, something has broken down badly. Ask an elder schooled in Afrika or the Caribbean about their relationship with their teachers and you will see the level of trust both parent and child had in their teachers. This trust was there because teachers were respected members of the local community, just behind the pastor, and because these Afrikan teachers genuinely loved and cared about the children in their care.

We have run into a problem in the so-called 'West' and as Afrikans all over the world have become Westernised (White thinking). My parents' generation learned the hard way that most Caucasian teachers had very little love or understanding for their Black students. My generation had bad experiences with Caucasian teachers in this country and transmitted this lack of trust and respect to your generation. Your generation, raised in a culture where children are encouraged to openly defy adult authority, does not hide these

...metimes expresses them in inappropriate ways.
...achers do not understand this history, these feelings and
... subconscious racism and many say your generation is
...able. Of course there were, are and always will be White
t...ers who genuinely care about and are committed to Afrikan
pupils, however as in all other walks of life there never were, never
are, or never will be; enough. Never Enough.

The real answer is Afrikan-centred schools, however in the short-
term you are going to have to do what I and many other Afrikans did,
which is to:

- Learn and accept that Teachers have more power than pupils,
- Seek fair treatment but don't expect it,
- Speak to your parents about any concerns you have in school,
- Keep out of bad company,
- Keep your head down and your eyes open
- Pass their exams.

Police – The Police, Babylon, Feds, Pigs, call them what you will,
have power. They have serious power. The power of life or death.
Don't ramp with the Police. They have the power to kill you or leave
you to die (see later chapter on Afrikan males and the Police) and the
chances are they will not even lose their jobs, let alone go to prison.

Jean Charles de Menezes was shot seven times in the head on the
London Underground for looking a bit 'Middle Eastern'. Remember,
several of the people convicted and/or accused of being suicide
bombers were Afrikans. **You could be in the firing line soon so be
careful.**

When dealing with the Police remember:

- They have the Power of the State behind them and can enforce it
  with, guns, batons, CS Gas, Tazar (electric shock device), dogs,
  handcuffs, leg restraints, water cannon, plastic bullets, the courts
  etc.
- They have a bigger gang than you will ever have,
- Stay calm and do not respond to provocation

- Note officers' numbers (usually on the shoulder or chest of their uniform)
- Do not raise your voice or gesticulate with your arms too much
- Know your rights if stopped in the street. Ask them politely to explain their actions

Employers – Sons of Afrika, understand this. Most employers are looking to employ people whom they consider to be likeminded. That is to say they are looking to employ people who think and act like them and share the same values. Most of them have a picture of their ideal employee deep in their subconscious mind and this person does not normally look like you. Now; some Caucasian employers are able to overcome their racial programming to some extent and deal with the fact that you do not look like them, however they still want you to **think** like them. Job interviews are processes where behind the obvious question of can you do the job, the real $64,000 questions the interviewers are asking are:

- Are you enough like me (in terms of value system)?
And
- Do I feel comfortable with you?

However because most of us have spent most of our lives in situations where White people have power over us we have learned to flex like a chameleon and change mental colours, depending upon the situation. The famous Afrikan-American intellectual WEB DuBois called this '*Double Consciousness*', two souls, two ways of thinking, one Afrikan, the other European, battling for dominance within the same body. In order to get on in the White workplace they demand that your European consciousness – the way you walk, talk, gesticulate, think, deal with people, how you eat etc. – comes to the fore.

It is very difficult for a conscious brother or sister to 'get on' in the European workplace without losing some of their integrity (being true to what you believe in), or losing their job. These are the compromises and hard decisions that a conquered people are forced to make.

LESSONS FOR AFRIKAN LIFE

1. You need to understand what power is and who wields it in society.
2. How do you (Son) feel about the fact that you belong to a conquered race? How can we get back on top? How did other people rise after being conquered e.g. Chinese.
3. You need to understand the difference between income and wealth and know how wealth is created/accumulated. Clue – Two ways are by creating a scarcity (lack) of something or meeting/creating a need for a product or service.
4. Do you have an idea of the career you wish to follow and how much you are likely to earn from this type of work?
5. Remember, Oprah Winfrey who is a billionaire and perhaps the richest Black woman in the world was refused entrance to an exclusive shop on Madison Avenue in New York and again to another expensive shop in Paris. On both occasions the explanation was that the staff in the shop did not recognise her. This means that her fame and wealth makes her 'human' and worthy of being treated like rich White people, but without these she would be just another N****r to the shop staff. Similarly, some of the most famous rappers make 'out of hours' appointments with these same designer shops to ensure they are guaranteed entrance and no doubt to save the shop the embarrassment of being seen to sell to 'those kind of people'.

Recommendations

1. As a family discuss the issue of power and look back in history at times when we exercised real Black Power.
2. Watch the news and discuss its content.
3. Listen to Afrikan-centred internet radio stations e.g. www.libradio.com www.gap-radio.com www.innerlightradio.com www.blakeradio.com for our point of view on world affairs.
4. Parents. If you don't already have one, make a family budget and discuss it with your son so he understands the family finances.
5. Sit down with your son and calculate your household's wealth.
6. Make sure your son has a savings account and saves money regularly. This is good discipline for adult life.
7. Go shopping with a list. 70% of purchases are made on impulse. A list helps to curb your impulses!

Recommended Reading:

Black Economics – Jawanza Kunjufu
Blueprint for Black Power – Amos N. Wilson
Niggers, Negroes, Black People and Afrikans – Paul Grant
Rich Dad, Poor Dad – Robert Kiyosaki and Sharon Lechter
The Road to Power – Keidi Obi Awadu

A Job vs. A Career

I was born in 1966 and when I was a child my parents, and my friends parents, used to tell me to 'Learn yu book and get a good job'. We were always being told to 'go read a book' as education was seen as the key to getting on in life.

Now whilst this was good advice, it was incomplete advice. Our parents grew up under European colonialism and learnt subconsciously that the most we could aspire to was to work for 'the White man'. If you look around your local community, or town or city you live in, you will notice that even in those parts of town where a lot of us live we own comparatively few businesses. You will notice that every few years new groups of non-Afrikan immigrants set up businesses in these areas and that these businesses rely on members of their community **and us** to support them. You will also notice that these new groups **do not** support our businesses.

Virtually every other group of people, particularly where they are a minority, teach their people to develop *a career* to look after themselves.

A career is different to having a job.
A career is about developing a range of knowledge, skills and experiences that will allow you to always be able to look after yourself and your family even if you lose your job. Having a career plan means that you will not be afraid to set up in business for yourself and you will see this as a positive and realistic option.

A job is about working for someone else and looking forward to retirement when you will finally be able to start enjoying yourself. A job mentality means that you will be terrified of losing that job and your White employer will be able to '*keep you under manners*' by simply threatening to take your job away.

Most Afrikan people have jobs. Most Afrikan people hate their jobs. If you don't believe me ask around. If you ask most of the Afrikans you know why they don't leave their jobs the main reasons will be:
• Money – pay is good

- Money – they can't afford to be out of work
- Fear – they don't know what they would do if they stopped working for White people
- Status – people look up to them if they have an important sounding job title
- Fear – they know that most Black people do not support Black businesses the way other groups support their own businesses. They also know that other groups boycott Black businesses

I understand all of the above since I have been there and got the T-shirt. I have experienced the financial fear, the emotional fear and the lack of self-confidence. I stopped working for White people in February 2006. It was scarey, but I have never felt happier and more fulfilled since I started working for myself, my family and my people full-time. This book is a product of that new found freedom and time. It took me 2 years to write my first book, 18months to write my second book and four months to write this book. That is not because I have not put time and effort into this book, it is because firstly, I now have more experience as a writer; and secondly, and more importantly, I no longer have to write late at night after working a ten hour day for someone else.

Be clear, I am not saying we should all give up our jobs overnight, I would lose my free supply of paper and envelopes if all Afrikans did that! But seriously, I am suggesting that we should all look at developing alternative ways of bringing in income to lesson our dependency upon 'the job' and that we should teach our children to view going into business/self-employment as a first not last option. There is a book 'Feel The Fear and Do it Anyway', by Susan Jeffers and we are going to have to think seriously about this and then act.

Recommendations

Sons – There are some things that you need to do to escape the Job mentality:

1. Study hard and understand the types of qualification needed for different types of career.

2. Develop an area of academic knowledge e.g. physicist, computer programmer and an area of vocational skill e.g. building, plumbing etc.

3. Make sure you are numerate (can deal confidently with numbers). Don't shirk mathematics and the sciences.

4. Understand that if Caucasians don't push you, and have low expectations of you, in certain areas e.g. Maths and Science, these are exactly the areas you should be looking at. We don't need any more singers, rappers, dancers, comedians, probation officers, social workers etc.

5. Discuss with your parents changes to the national and worldwide economy. What types of skills will be in demand in the economy in the next 10-15 years.

6. Remember in a capitalistic economy you make money by having a skill that is scarce and in demand. That is to say the less people who have your skill the more you can charge for this skill.

For parents:

1. Don't rely on careers advisors to point your children in the right direction.

2. Discuss your work history honestly with your son and discuss what you would do differently if you had a second chance.

3. Look at how you can improve your career prospects whatever your income level or success.

Recommended Reading:

Powernomics – Claude Anderson
Think and Grow Rich, A Black Choice – Dennis Kimbro and Napoleon Hill

Is my Mum Ugly? The seemingly irresistible attraction of the White girl/woman

'The White woman is the Black man's Krytonite'
Film – Undercover Brother

"Next to God we are indebted to women, first for life itself, and then for making it worth living."
Mary McLeod Bethune

What would I mean if I said that most Afrikan people have a '*White Beauty Ideal*' and this was one of the main reasons that most Black boys/young men in the UK, who have girlfriends, go out with White girls/young women and why if they do go out with Black girls/young women they prefer them light skinned with long hair?

Well, a people's beauty ideal is the perfect image of female beauty in their collective minds. Not everyone thinks the same, however it represents those physical characteristics that the people from that group generally find most attractive.

There is a lot of self-deception and hypocrisy in the Black community about beauty. In the 1960's we used to say "Our skin is Black, our hair is curly, our noses are broad, our lips are thick and we are beautiful". That was us trying to convince ourselves. We said it because we really believed that we were ugly...and we still do! To be more precise we dislike anything that reminds us that we are Afrikan. Therefore the more typically Afrikan you look the lower you are on this insane beauty scale.

One of the greatest achievements of White Racism was to create a world where many people believe that:

White = Good
Black = Bad
White = Beautiful
Black = Ugly
God = White
(D)Eve(il) = Black

Male = Good
Female = Bad

The warped beauty of racism is that not only does it cause most White people to believe that they are superior, but it leads most Black people to believe that we are inferior.

Sociologist Robert Staples notes that "Given that many Black men prefer their women light or White, the supply of such women is limited for a number of reasons. ...When the Roper organization asked Black and white men what qualities are most admired in a woman, the Black males ranked sex appeal fourth – White males ranked it sixth. When *Jet* magazine surveyed Black males in Chicago on the ten things they most notice about women, they listed in this order (1) face (2) legs (3) bust (4) eyes-hair (5) personality (6) dress intelligence (7) smile (8) buttocks (9) walk (10) hands-feet-conversation-sincerity." (Staples in Hare and Hare 1989: 72)

Staples goes on to suggest that "...the first four physical traits are generally most common to white women. The face should be light and keen in features, legs and bust should be big, eyes round, hair long and straight." (Staples in Hare and Hare 1989: 72)

So there we have it, what we have known for a long time. Many Afrikan men with Afrikan partners on a subconscious psychological level are simply seeking Caucasian women with a bit of skin melanin. Of course, nowadays, particularly in places such as the UK where there is a ready supply of available White women, many more are dropping the pretence and simply opting for the real McCoy i.e. the Caucasian woman.

The sister depicted in the promotional flyer below represents the current 'Black beauty Ideal'. She passes the *brown paper bag* test i.e. she is lighter than a brown paper bag and her hair blows in the wind. In a very real sense she represents our hatred of being Afrikan. It is not that light skinned sisters should not be presented as Black beauty ideals, it is rather that it should not **always** be light skinned sisters. I am in no way attempting to deny her beauty or Blackness, but rather to tell it like it is and say that you never see a dark skinned sister with short natural hair, broad nose and thick lips on such a flyer. You know its true don't you. The truth is that the dark skinned sister just described will often get more sexual interest from White men than Black men.

On the day I decided to include the above picture in this book I spoke to an 11 year old Afrikan boy about beauty concepts and relationships. Among the many interesting things he said was that virtually all of the Afrikan boys at his school expressed a preference for White or Mixed Race girls. That is why I like children. They are honest. He also went on to say that some of these boys went for the Mixed Race girls because their Mums had warned them off White girls.

The above flyer also highlights the presentation of Afrikan women as sex objects by Afrikan men which is a consistent theme in these types of flyers, Black music magazines etc.

Point for Son to discuss with Parent – Do you date Caucasian girls and if so why? If you don't date Afrikan girls, why not? Discuss the relative attractiveness of Afrikan and Caucasian females.

The following quotes (my comments in bold) from a report published in the UK in 2006 highlights what I have been warning

Afrikan people about regarding inter-racial relationships (see my two previous books). Whether you believe love is colour-blind is irrelevant. The plain truth is that if the ever increasing rate of Afrikans (particularly of Caribbean descent) in the UK 'marrying/partnering out' continues there will be no hope for Black people in the UK (and in the US if Afrikans over there don't take note).

....Caribbean and white women are broadly similar in their fertility rates. But, while one in ten white women with children (and under 35) is a single mother, no less than half of Caribbean mothers are single (never-married) parents.

Lesson – **Single parent households are more likely to live in poverty**

The combination of the low rates of partnership, high rates of single parenthood, and high rates of mixed marriage means that only a quarter of 'Caribbean' children live with two black parents.

Lesson – **Mashed up families produce mashed up communities**

The key feature of family life in the Caribbean community is the low rate of marriage. Caribbeans are less likely to live with a partner than white people; those who have a partner are less likely to have married them; those who have married are more likely to separate or divorce.

Lesson – **We need to teach our sons how to make relationships work and the value of marriage**

Among British-born Caribbeans, half of men with a partner live with a white woman; a third of women with a partner live with a white man. The rate of mixed partnership is increasing rapidly for men (though not for women).

Learn this: Social Integration = Social Disintegration = Biological Elimination (for minorities)

Family formation in multi-cultural Britain: three patterns of diversity1 *Richard Berthoud, Institute for Social and Economic*

Research, University of Essex (2006)

There is no clearer representation of this self-hatred than in the following advert which was taken from the ironically titled UK publication 'Black Hair and Beauty' in the Dec 2004/Jan 2005 edition. The irony is no doubt lost on the Negroes who publish this magazine and actually believe that their various representations of Afrikan women make some positive contribution to our people's sense of self worth. Look at the following advert and judge for yourself. This is called 'internalised racism'.

This is the 21st century version of Negro/Ni***r beauty. What is more disturbing? The fact that thousands of Afrikan women buy this magazine and obviously either support the use of these products (the manufacturers produce these products to satisfy a demand), do not care enough about this gross insult to boycott the magazine or complain, or that the Afrikans who publish this magazine care so little about their people that they will accept these types of adverts, which I am sure they are aware can only do damage to the Afrikan mind.

It is not just the Swiss cashing in on this vibrant and ever growing market in self-hatred. Many of these skin bleaching products are manufactured in Nigeria and exported all over West Afrika as well as further afield. Here in Nottingham, where I live, you see Jamaican women in particular, but by no means exclusively, sporting the unmistakeably ghastly, pinky bleached face look with accompanying naturally dark skinned hands and feet. Zombie would a fraid a dem.

Of course one has only to watch any music video to see that the *Brown paper bag rule* of Black beauty – which states that a Black woman should be no darker than those brown paper shopping bags that are common in the US and that her hair should blow in the wind – is still in full effect. This is the more subtle yet dangerous side of Afrikan self hatred.

Just for the record. The active ingredient in most of these skin bleaching agents is the compound hydroquinone. The maximum recommended 'dose' in the UK is 1% by volume. After suffering a bad bout of chicken pox in my early twenties I was prescribed a product called 'Fade Out' by my doctor to apply to the areas of most severe scarring on my face resulting from the chicken pox. I can remember checking the label and noting it had 1% hydroquinone by volume. I also remember that my doctor advised me to use it for no more than six weeks. It is worth noting that some of the skin bleaching agents produced in Nigeria and other countries have up to 5% hydroquinone by volume.

Hydroquinone is a carcinogenic (cancer causing) chemical – like many other chemical compounds – and even at the 1% level should be considered dangerous. When you think of the prolonged and liberal use of these products by Afrikan women one can only dread to think of the health problems that they are storing up for themselves.

I suppose it is like the Caucasian woman who when warned of the dangers of skin cancer associated with sunbathing commented 'well at least I will be a good looking corpse'. For too many Afrikan women the prize of light skin is obviously worth risking cancer for.

We are *functionally mentally ill* (Grant 2003) and the worst thing is that most of us don't even know it.

Black Women and their Hair

Questions for Sons to discuss with Mum:

Why is hair so important to Afrikan women and why do they spend so much time and money on it?

Why do most Afrikan women either chemically straighten (so-called relaxing and perming) their hair or wear false hair i.e. wigs, weaves and extensions?

Why is it that increasing numbers of Afrikan women are using chemical dyes to make their hair look blonde or at the least a lot lighter in colour?

Is the above all about convenience, self hatred or a combination of the two?

Does Black women trying to get their hair to look like White women's send a message to their sons that the White woman is the measure of true beauty?

"… few things generate more anger and passion among black women than their hair. Some black critics say that black women are in a frenzied search to shed the ancient racist shame and stigma of "nappy hair" ="bad hair" by aping white beauty standards. Others say that, like many non-black women, black women are hopeless captives of America's fashion and beauty industry, which is geared to making them more attractive and pleasing to men. Many black women counter this by saying that they are merely seeking their own identity or "to look better.

A century ago the legendary Madame CJ Walker built a multi-million dollar empire on the premise that black women want to look like white women and that "good hair" is the key to independence and prosperity.

"Elegance, spiced with Southern flavor begins with a mane awash in a light golden blond shade."

The great hair obsession is driven by the painful need of many African-Americans to conform to the dominant values of American society. And beauty, fashion and hairstyles are the most popular and perverse expressions of those values. .....many African-Americans still believe the fiction that good hair makes you, and nappy hair doesn't."

Earl Ofari Hutchinson (1998 Afrocentric News "*The Crisis in Black and Black*")

I know one sister who; when she 'went natural' and cut her hair, was greeted with shock and dismay by her mother and sisters. I am absolutely convinced that if she had greeted them in a full length blonde wig she would have received a more enthusiastic, supportive response. It was so sad that one of her sisters was actually suffering significant hair loss at the time – as a result of the peroxide based chemicals used in hair straighteners – but refused to even give her hair a break to recover from this chemical attack, such was her addiction to the idea of straight hair. Ironically, she was the family member most hostile to her sibling 'going natural'.

Similarly, I can recall when I worked in schools there was an Afrikan girl who was called 'toast' and other insults by some of the self-hating little Negroes who my generation are raising up, due to her lovely dark skin. When she had her hair chemically straightened another girl said to her, by way of a compliment, "your hair looks decent now". Of course she still continued to be insulted by her schoolmates based upon her dark complexion.

It is incredible to me, but sadly true, that it actually takes courage for an Afrikan woman to walk in this world with her own hair, and nothing but her hair (including chemical straightners), so help her ancestors.

Am I being a little harsh? Perhaps, especially since the psychological pressure to 'lighten and lengthen' Afrikan hair is everywhere. Afrikan girls as young as four or five are saying that they hate their hair. If they were saying they hated their skin colour we would see it as a major problem (I hope), however I guess it is difficult for many Afrikan mothers to speak authoritatively against such sentiments from their daughters since they themselves are constantly battling with their own 'hair psychosis'.

BEAUTY LESSONS FOR AFRIKAN LIFE

Points to discuss based upon the information contained in this chapter:

1. Mother/Father – What beauty ideal does your son see his mother chasing/imitating and what message does it send to him?
2. Does anyone in your family talk about 'good hair'. If so, discuss this with your son.
3. How many males in your extended family have non-Afrikan partners? Why do you think these people chose their partners?
4. Is love really colour blind? If so why do Afrikans marry out at a far higher rate than other racial/ethnic groups?
5. Why are nearly all of the models featured on the front cover of Black women's magazines light skinned with long straight hair or chemically altered hair?
6. Why do most men from nearly all other racial/ethnic group choose women who look like their mothers, but increasingly Afrikan men do not? **Are our mothers ugly?**

Recommendations

For sons :

1. Choose an Afrikan/Black girlfriend
2. Follow the golden rule – Treat your girlfriend the way you would want a man to treat your Mum, Sister, Aunt, Cousin etc.
3. Compliment sisters who keep their hair natural i.e. no chemicals, wigs, weaves etc. This will help Black girls/women to love their Afrikan selves

For parents:

1. Discuss with your son the concept of Beauty and issues such as shadeism in the Afrikan community
2. Mums – Don't get mad with me, but why not 'go natural' with your hair.
3. Tell your son that you expect him to bring home someone who looks like his Mum.

Recommended Reading/Viewing

Crisis in Black Sexual Politics – eds. Nathan and Julia Hare
Brazil: Mixture or Massacre? – Abdias Do Nascimento
Niggers, Negroes, Black People and Afrikans – Paul Grant
Killing "Me" $oftly: Death by Assimilation – Abdullah Nazir Uhuru
Undercover Brother (DVD)
Sankofa (DVD) – Haile Gerima

Homosexuality and other forms of sexual degeneracy in the Afrikan community

"We shall sodomize your sons....we shall seduce them in your schools, in your dormitories, in your gymnasiums, in your locker rooms, in your sports arenas, in your seminaries, in your movie theatre bathrooms, in your army bunkhouses, in your truck stops, in your all male clubs, in your houses of congress.....your sons will do our bidding. They will be recast in our image. They will come to crave and adore us.

(Gene Antonio, "AIDS: A Weapon in the Hands of Militant Homosexuals," Intercessors for America newsletter, June 1987, p.2. cited in Baruti 2003: 76)

Introduction

Of all the chapters in this book, this is probably the one that will be viewed as the most controversial and that will generate the greatest hostile and negative comments. We have to ask ourselves why this is? Thirty years ago such a chapter would not have generated the same reaction. That was a time when firstly, Caucasians were not so confident in fully expressing their sexual selves to the wider non-Caucasian world, and secondly, Afrikans were not as assimilated into European culture as we are today.

In discussing attitudes to various forms of sexual behaviour in the Afrikan community it is important to note that, certainly in 'the West', and increasingly in Afrika, these attitudes are almost wholly copied and imported from the White 'liberal' community which dominates large sections of the electronic media (TV, radio, cinema) and the public sector organisations where many Afrikans work. Negroes, who are at the forefront of persuading Afrikans to become more European in their attitudes to sex, are also at the forefront of trying to 'Blackenise' European sexual perversion to make it acceptable to Black people.

Readers should, indeed must, understand that a people's attitude to sex stems from their culture which is the basis of their worldview. It is as simple as that. There is nothing objective or 'normal' about the

European view of sex. It is simply the European view of sex. Nothing more, nothing less.

Sex as Progress

What has sex got to do with progress? Well, Europeans are obsessed with the idea of 'progress'. Progress for them means anything new and different regardless of whether it is beneficial to society or not. For most people from other cultures progress means positive change that helps society. It is important to recognise this difference.

When it comes to sex Europeans get bored very quickly and bring their idea of progress into the equation. This means that as a cultural group they are always looking for new forms of sex to experiment with. Very early in their history the idea of men and women having 'standard' sex became considered very boring and traditional – they consider tradition as negative. Europeans have 'progressed' sexually to the point where the following sexualised behaviours are now considered 'normal' in 'Western' culture: Homosexuality, Bisexuality, Bondage/Sadomasochism, Transvestism, Transsexualism.

Given this European idea of 'sexual progress' I predicted in my last book 'Blue Skies for Afrikans' that Adult Incest and Bestiality would become increasingly acceptable in mainstream (they have always been widely practiced by Europeans) European sexual culture in the next 20-30 years. There is not space in this book to provide the evidence to support this claim, however I provided material to support my ideas in my last book so you can check it out there if you need convincing.

European sexual 'progress' is a road to nowhere. It leads to ever more bizarre, alienated and despiritualised forms of sexual practice. Participants are forever reaching for the stars and coming up empty handed. It can only lead to ever increasing levels of relationship break up, emotional isolation and social fragmentation. Europeans want to throw their cloak of sexual culture over the entire planet to normalise their madness. For them the outlandish soon becomes normal. For rightminded Afrikans this is sickness and we need to keep well out of it.

So what should be our attitude to homosexuality and other forms

74

of abnormal sexual practice? Well, firstly let's define normality. Professor Wade Nobles defines normality as:

"Normal behaviour can be defined as life giving or life affirming behaviour."
Professor Wade Nobles

Mwalimu K Bomani Baruti who has written probably the most comprehensive Afrocentric book on homosexuality 'Homosexuality and the Effeminization of Afrikan Males' tells us:

"Accepting homosexuality simply because it is in the family is too simplistic a solution for an intelligent people. Many of us grew up in the same household with individuals who were accused of and served time for serious felonies. That does not compel us to take up a life of crime. Too many of us have had our blood contaminated by European rape. But we do not, or at least should not, condone the rapist. All of us are biologically linked to negroes, or someone who physically or mentally abuses their spouse or tortures themselves with legal and/or illegal drugs.

Lesson – **A behaviour should not be considered normal just because a lot of people engage in it.**

That should not guide us to become negroes, mentally or physically abuse our loved ones, or destroy our minds and bodies with drugs. Loving a relative is not the same as loving or embracing what s/he does. Just because you love a relative does not mean you are supposed to embrace what they do, or go out and do what they do. Loving the person is not the same as loving or liking what s/he does. That's like assuming that because you have a son or daughter, or brother or sister, who is a prostitute that you should love prostitution, and/or accept or pursue it as a worthy occupation. That's like assuming that because you have a family member in the military you should support Western wars against the world. On the other hand, obviously, most people have an Afrikan warrior scholar in their family. Yet, they are not embracing it or, ofttimes, even him or her.

Lesson – **Afrikans are quick to embrace those things that**

Europeans tell us are acceptable. Hence why so few embrace Afrocentrism.

So what is the criteria being used to pick and choose those more unpopular (undesirable) qualities we select to embrace or try to become like. Obviously, they are those which will make for an easier assimilation into whiteness. Those socialized and/or genocultural qualities or personality traits which encourage and facilitate Afrikan manhood do not. Those which de-emphasize it at least offer the possibility.

Lesson: Europeans are hostile to the development of strong Afrikan-centred men. Many Afrikans are desperate to be accepted by Europeans therefore unconsciously suppress/discourage Afrikan manhood and encourage cultural assimilation.

We must remember that mentacidal conditions are the result of illnesses created within the constraints of white supremacist culture. The choices Afrikans make occur within these constraints. As we know, if you swim in a sea of perversity you are bound to get wet. Therefore, if for no other reason, we should never argue that these behaviors should be embraced by the Afrikan community just because there is a number of family members whom are mentacidal enough to think or act that way."

Lesson – **Minimise your social and cultural contact with Caucasians or Afrikans with European minds if you wish to avoid getting 'wet' in their culture of sexual perversion. If this is your family, just do your best to keep it Black!**

Mwalimu K. Bomani Baruti *Homosexuality and the Effeminization of Afrikan Males* (2003)

Sex and Violence

Europeans have a long history of associating consensual sex and violence. It is important to be clear here that we are not talking about rape. Take time out to review television programmes. Just watch and see how often Europeans link passionate sex with violence. How often have you seen men and women throwing each other up against walls, tearing each other's clothes off, scratching, gnawing and biting at each other, all as part of supposed lovemaking. You probably don't even react to these scenes because they are so frequent that you become desensitised to such acts, however there is nothing normal about this type of behaviour. These acts are rooted in European culture.

A classic example of violent European sex is in the first Basic Instinct film made in the mid 1990's. In the scene in question the lead male character played by Michael Douglas (a self-confessed sex addict in real life) goes around to his sometime sexual partner's, and police psychologist, house. As soon as she opens the door he pushes her back and plays out a violent sexual scene in which he eventually throws her over a piece of furniture and has intercourse with her from behind. It is a scene that is full of violence and which sends out some highly dangerous messages about female consent in sex. There is absolutely no emotional intimacy or tenderness. In effect Michael Douglas uses the woman like a toilet, to masturbate in, since his only connection to her is physical.

The whole film is a classic study in European sexual culture and morality. The lead female character played by Sharon Stone is a psychopath who murders her male victims by stabbing them at the moment of sexual climax. She also engages in female homosexuality (mistakenly referred to as lesbianism). Despite knowing that she is the chief suspect in these murders, the Michael Douglas character, who is an alcoholic, has sex with her whilst conducting his investigations. The most famous scene in the film and the one that guaranteed its box office success, was set at a police station, where under questioning from an unusually large number of male detectives, Sharon Stone, who is wearing a short skirt, uncrosses and crosses her legs to reveal a glimpse of her pubic hair to the detectives (and the camera of course). This scene is about her using sex as a means to gain psychological power over men as well as providing a controversial moment that guaranteed box office success.

The whole film intertwines sex and violence and promotes the idea that sex is a battle for power and that one party must exercise control over the other. Of course when the Sharon Stone and Michael Douglas characters have sex it is filled with violence and the anticipation of violence. In fact the Michael Douglas character is positively turned on by the idea that the Sharon Stone character has murdered men during the sexual act. It all adds to the excitement!

The Role of Television

Television is at the forefront of promoting and normalising European sexual culture or 'White Sex'. In line with their obsession with progress you will notice that Caucasians are obsessed with 'sexual firsts' on television. First naked full frontal image of a woman, first erect male penis on TV, first homosexual kiss on television, first graphic depiction of oral sex, first graphic simulated depiction of anal sex, and so on. Of course once they achieve one milestone they have to move onto the next. There is no end possible since of course to stop these firsts would mean an end of progress in the European mind. They even have programmes celebrating the breaking down of these taboos.

As in so many things, entertainment is used as the vehicle to break down and change moral values and social attitudes. As Gobbels, Hitler's Minister of Propoganda, told Nazi filmmakers, whilst dismissing their serious documentary films as useless for Nazi propaganda, "Put it in entertainment" and so they did. Most people don't like watching documentaries and if they do watch them tend to concentrate and think about the content. On the other hand most people do like watching comedies and/or soap operas and tend to relax and 'switch off' whilst watching them leaving them more vulnerable to the values being promoted in these programmes.

There is an incredible onslaught of programming promoting homosexuality, sado-masochism, heterosexual anal sex, rimming, golden showers, bestiality, and all other manner of sexual perversion on television. Most of this stuff is so frequent it passes without comment. Much of this programming is on before the watershed (9.00pm in the UK) and most of it is in 'entertainment' programmes. Just a few examples: Coronation Street (transsexualism, homosexuality etc.) which is broadcast at 7.30pm and repeated in the afternoons on Sundays, Eastenders (early promoter of male homosexuality and more recently, 2006, female homosexuality [involving an Afrikan] etc) is broadcast at 7.30pm and repeated on

Sunday afternoons, Friends (every form of sexual perversion you can imagine via jokes and accepting comments rather than explicit acts) which is seemingly repeated at every hour you can think of in the UK, Just Shoot Me (very similar to Friends except with even more frequent sexual references), Will & Grace (Male Homosexuality at its core).

Despite being the home of a pornographic industry that is bigger than Hollywood, terrestrial television in the US is more restrained than in the UK and I think US viewers would be shocked by what is broadcast by UK terrestrial channels, particularly Channel 4 and Channel 5.

Finally, make a note of the number of Afrikan men dressing up as women on television and film. Two of the biggest cinema box office hits of 2005/2006 involved Afrikan men dressing up as Afrikan women. Martin Lawrence loves it so much he repeated his role in the film 'Big Mama 2', which of course presents, middle aged Afrikan women as ugly, foul mouthed figures of fun. These characterisations – especially of dark-skinned Afrikan women – were first seen in films such as 'Gone with The Wind' (with the verbal crudity not yet developed) and the Black maid character whose face you never see in the Tom & Jerry cartoons.

Transvestism has been a part of European entertainment culture since the earliest days of European theatre when they had men dressing up as women to play female roles, such was their level of sexism. You see this tradition continued in pantomimes for children where women dress up as men and men dress up as women and you now increasingly see this trend in films. Be clear, transvestism is linked to homosexuality and transsexualism.

Prisons as a Breeding Ground for Homosexuality

'Abnormal environments create abnormal behaviour' and prisons are one of the most abnormal environments created by Caucasians. I say Caucasians, because prisons were created by Caucasians in the 19th century although they had developed a taste for locking people up long before then. Everywhere around the world people have followed this trend without ever stopping to ask, how did we get to this point and what did we do before prisons?

Take a look at caged animals in a zoo. You will often see them pacing back and forth repetitively, with no purpose and no interest in the world around. This is a clear sign of mental distress through being kept in an abnormal environment.

If you put together the most violent people in society, many of whom have been emotionally, physically and some sexually abused, together in a big cage and without intensive counselling and support, what do you expect to get except abnormal behaviour?

Many of the men and women in prison are not particularly dangerous, however some prisoners are extremely dangerous predators and they do not stop attacking weaker people once they are locked up. There is very little talk about the large amount of rape and sexual assault that takes place in prisons, not to mention consensual homosexuality, which is hardly surprising and yet we know it is taking place, by the day, by the hour, by the minute, by the second.

The massive warehousing of Afrikan men in prisons is one of the greatest causes of the increase in homosexuality in the Afrikan community in Caucasian societies. There are an unbelievable 1.3 million Afrikan men in US prisons and this is a conservative estimate based upon federal prisons. In the UK the numbers are much smaller – 16% of a total prison population of 78,000 – but growing rapidly. Just as important are the increasing sentence lengths, since increased sentences will lead to further community disintegration and increased homosexuality.

In Iran male prisoners are allowed conjugal visits from their wives since the Iranians are aware of the points I have made regarding the effects of an abnormal environment upon human sexuality. Women are hardly ever imprisoned in Iran.

Conclusion

There are some myths about homosexuality and other forms of sexual degeneracy that Europeans and their cultural followers love to promote. Unfortunately, due to the size of this book I do not have room to discuss these issues in detail here. I will simply have to note them and ask you to read the recommended books if you want more detailed information and evidence to support my claims. These myths include:

- Homosexuality has Afrikan origins – There is no evidence of Afrikan homosexuality prior to Arab and European invasions.
- Homosexuality has a genetic basis – This is a speculation and there is no firm evidence to support it. Also this still would not make it normal from an Afrikan perspective. Europeans are claiming a genetic basis for everything from violence (guess who they say has more of these genes) to drug addiction. Does that make these things 'normal'? There is some evidence that 'endocryine disrupting chemicals' may be having an effect on human sexuality.
- Male Homosexuality is unconnected to the sexual abuse of boys. There is a lot of evidence that boys who have been sexually abused suffer severe confusion and anxiety over their sexuality since society leads them to believe that 'real men don't get raped' (unless you are Ving Rhames in Pulp Fiction) and therefore they often come to believe that they must have subconsciously wanted to have sex with a man and must therefore be homosexual. Sexual abuse is probably the biggest single cause of male homosexuality.
- Homosexuals are born not created – This relates to the above points. There is evidence of a significant growth in homosexuality amongst Afrikan men in 'the West'. This cannot be genetic since human genes do not change in a few decades therefore it is social in origin. As mentioned above, sexual abuse can create homosexuality as well as a sexually obsessed culture which promotes sexual experimentation such as we see in the Caucasian world and where Afrikans are obsessed with every form of integration. Given that we know that the average paedophile abuses dozens if not hundreds of children in their lifetime you can see the effects this will have.

N.B. It should be noted that 'endocryine disrupting chemicals' are having a drastic effect on human biology and are affecting fertility (male sperm count has fallen by 50% in 'the West' since the second 'European War on the World') cancer rates and no doubt sexuality. These changes are a product of organic mutation due to chemical attack and are not natural to the human condition.

- Homosexuality frees women from stereotyped roles – The remarkable thing one finds with so many homosexual relationships is their rather strange attempts to reproduce a stereotyped male/female relationship. What I mean by this is that in many female homosexual relationships you find one woman playing the role of 'man' – sometimes referred to as Bull Dykes – whilst the other plays the role of 'woman'. This madness was brought home clearly when a news report into the passing into statute of the new 'Civil Partnerships' bill in the UK showed a female homosexual couple who had just got 'married', one wearing a traditional male tuxedo wedding outfit whilst her partner was dressed in a traditional European white wedding dress. On the surface this may seem bizarre, however it makes sense if you understand that these homosexuals are subconsciously seeking to achieve the balance of feminine and masculine energy – that underpins the universe – that they consciously reject in their choice of sex partners. Similarly, in male homosexual relationships you often find the 'man' (giver) and 'woman' (receiver). It is also worth noting that there is a high level of domestic violence reported in female homosexual relationships.

Lessons for Afrikan Life – Recommendations

For parents:

1. Speak to your son about sex and sexuality. Be clear about what your view is and the rationale for it.
2. Be careful about any men under whose authority you place your son e.g. football teams, church choir, boy's brigade, mentoring or rites of passage programmes etc. Sexual abusers are attracted to where they can find their prey.
3. Understand that many Afrikans do not promote an Afrikan worldview or cultural viewpoint. If you can possibly avoid it do not place your son in the care of anyone, Afrikan or not who promotes European culture. Be aware your son's school is designed to promote European culture unless it is an independent Afrikan school.
4. Watch some of your son's favourite TV programmes with him and discuss the sexual imagery and messages.

For sons:
1. Understand that your school will promote a European view of sex and sexuality to you. Do not try to fight them, you cannot win this argument. Go home and talk to your parent(s) and other significant responsible Afrikan adults.
2. Don't believe that any type of sexual behaviour is 'normal' just because a lot of people practice it. There are only two sexual organs, the penis and vagina. "Human physiology clearly establishes that the mouth and the anus are not designed for sex." (Dr Llaila O. Afrika : xvii cited in Baruti 2003) Sexualisation of other parts of the body comes out of a cultural context.
3. Stay out of prison.

Recommended Reading

Homosexuality and the Effeminization of Afrikan Males – Mwalimu K Bomani Baruti
Blue Skies for Afrikans – Paul Ifayomi Grant
The Endangered Black Family – Nathan and Julia Hare
War on the Horizon: Black Resistance to the White Sex Assault – Positive Kemetic Visions

Ho's, Bitches and Shiners –
The music and Language of Hate

'Never curse the womb from whence you came'
Afrikan proverb

'The World is full of women and their children'

Why do increasing numbers of Afrikan boys seem to lack respect for females? One of the – but not the only – contributory factors is the degradation of Black music. You must have noticed how the disrespecting of girls and women has become an almost required part of what used to be called 'Black' and which has now been renamed; 'Urban' music. This Misogyny (hatred of women) is also common in Heavy Metal music, although it gets its highest media coverage when featured in rap and dancehall music.

Watch almost any US rap video and you have the obligatory 'video ho's' as they are known, shaking their shapely booties and breasts in the camera which then pans across to some ignorant, miseducated young man holding his penis, surrounded by his 'crew', often whilst driving or leaning on a luxury (rented) car, wearing expensive (rented) jewellery whilst he and his bredren tell you how they 'smoked a n*g**r' then 'f**ked a b*t*h, then got high on weed and how all that matters is being 'respected', 'keeping it real' and 'getting paid'.

The women are treated like pieces of meat, to be jabbed, poked, screwed etc. etc. and are portrayed in the lyrics of these records as sneaky, greedy, untrustworthy, and generally unworthy of even the slightest respect.

Some of the so-called Black community is full of hypocrisy in defending the slackness, stupidity and nastiness that comes out of the mouths of these young men. Whilst they are quick to bawl about racism they make excuses to defend the woman hating sexism that runs throughout these records.

Many of these 'artists' are hypocrites. Dr Dre is happily married and freely admits that he never refers to his wife as a bitch or ho and that he went back to 'gangsta rap' because his record sales fell after he cleaned up his act. Similarly Ja Rule whose lyrics are featured below is also married and I bet he does not speak to his wife in the way he raps about women.

Parent and son discussion point – Read the JaRule lyrics below and discuss how each of you feels about the way women are described. Ask your son how he would feel if his Mum, sister, or daughter (when he has children) were described in this way by a man. Ask your son if he ever refers to girls as bitches, ho's, shiners etc. If yes, ask him to explain why he does it.

Ja Rule
I'll F*** U Girl (Skit)
Tell 'em
Reemo.....Distribution
Well, you know what we'll do....tell 'em (baby)
You know I.......(whachya gonna do now?)
Fuck ya girl!
Face down ass up
You know we like to
Fuck ya girl!
In the middle of the night
Put it in your butt
You know what's up I'll
Fuck ya girl!
If the puss gets dry
And the bitch gotta curl
Rub it in ya hair
I wanna
Fuck ya girl!
With my dick in her mouth
Chokin' her out (err)
Still gonna
Fuck ya girl!
(Hahaha!)
(This mother fucker's straight)
That's right, come on now!

All you bitches
Ain't give me no pussy before in here
Ya know what I'd say?
Oh, I ain't mad at you (That shit's gonna cost you)
Tina? You know what I'd do?
I'm gonna fuck you girl! (A thousand dollars)
Sherry? I'm gonna fuck you girl! (A thousand dollars)
Maria? I'm gonna fuck you girl! (A thousand dollars)
Lisa? I'm gonna fuck you girl! (A thousand dollars)
Haha!
Those bitches across the world
I'm gonna fuck you girl!
(Wait a minute! You mother fucking talkin' all that shit
That shit's comin' out your budget
Them hoes cost a thousand dollars a piece
Young ass nigger
But ya still my artist, baby king!
Ladies and gentlemen, baby king!
Ladies and gentlemen, god bless and good night.
I wanna goddamn thank all the mother fuckers
who put this together, my mother fucking self.
Anybody who question me...hmm, hold on
Where's my mother fucking bouncers?)

Now read the article below which is about how a hip hop magazine 'The Source' tried to expose Eminem's racism.

Diversity News: Dec. 20
DiversityInc.com

Court Stops Magazine From Distributing Racist Eminem Tape
A court ruling has stopped hip-hop magazine *The Source* from distributing a CD of a previously unreleased recording by rapper Eminem that includes phrases such as "black girls are dumb." Manhattan federal Judge Gerald Lynch granted Eminem's lawyers an injunction preventing the magazine from enclosing the CD in its

February issue, which goes on sale in mid-January. The magazine had planned extensive coverage of the recording.

Eminem's lawyers had argued that distributing the CD violates copyright laws.

The Source said it exposed the Eminem track while investigating the forces corrupting hip-hop, including racism. Last month, *The Source* held a news conference to accuse Eminem, who is white, of racism, citing lyrics on the recording such as "black girls are dumb, and white girls are good chicks."

The 31-year-old rapper has said the recording was "foolishness" that he'd made as a teen "out of anger, stupidity and frustration" after breaking up with a black girlfriend. Besides winning several Grammys, Eminem won an Oscar this year for his song "Lose Yourself" from the film "8 Mile." (Associated Press)

Now, why should anyone be surprised that Eninem is racist? Because he hangs around with Black rappers and 'acts Black' in his musical career? Eninem is a White man raised in a racist society just like other White men. Mick Jagger and the Rolling Stones also made an early recording with racist lyrics about Black women. It's all part of White's musical tradition. Elvis was a racist and Eninem admitted he was the new Elvis i.e. the new White boy put forward as the 'King' of Black music.

The Source is typical of the hypocrisy and sexism that runs throughout most of so-called Hip-Hop culture. They are quick to jump on Eninem for his comparatively mild expressions of racism but turn a blind eye to the mountain of hateful sexist crap put out by Afrikan rap artists, day in day out.

Some of the Effects of Sexism on Black Women

You may have heard it said that if you call someone stupid often enough they will believe it and we as Afrikan people have been called stupid and made to feel stupid for the longest time by Caucasians. In early 2006 a Leeds University lecturer, Frank Ellis, said that Afrikans were intellectually inferior to Caucasians and the White media gave him plenty of coverage and misguided Negroes joined in the discussion, thereby confirming that it was a point worth debating in their minds.

Similarly, if you call Black women ho's for long enough some of them will start to believe it and act like ho's. This process is called the *internalisation of oppression*.

Take a look at the pictures that follow. These were taken from US high school prom night photographs. I should make it clear I am not attacking these young sisters (one of the three sisters has kept some of her dignity). They are probably aged no more than eighteen and are a symptom of the problem, not the problem itself. The problem is how sexism and a society which is sexually obsessed turns young women into joints of meat (breasts, buttocks, thighs, calves, stomach etc.) and encourages them to present themselves in this way.

If you have ever had sight of the many dancehall videos/DVDs emanating out of Jamaica, New York etc. you will know that the young women in the following pictures are dressed comparatively modestly when compared to the unpaid 'stars' of these videos.

Clothes are part of what is known as *'symbolic language'* i.e. they allow you to say something about who you are without speaking.

Questions for Afrikan Life
1. Parent(s) and Son – What message do you think these young women are trying to send out to the world and what message do you think they are actually sending out?
2. Son – How would you feel if your Mum, Sister, Auntie, Cousin etc. went out dressed like these young women?
3. Why do you think the way women dress has changed and become more sexualised over the years?

Recommendations

Sons:

1. Learn and practice the golden rule: Treat all women the way you would like your Grandmother, Mother, Sister, Auntie, Cousin etc to be treated by men. This rule will always work unless you hate or disrespect your female relatives.

2. Never use violence against a woman except in the most serious situation to defend your life or someone else's life. If a girl or woman is 'winding you up' walk away.

3. Don't call women by hateful names such as bitch. If you call a woman a bitch then does that make you a son of a bitch? This language of hate is anti-Afrikan and remember what goes around comes around. If you put hate into the world you will eventually get hate back with interest!

Parents:

1. Monitor the media your son listens to and watches. Sit down with him and discuss sexism in TV adverts, films, videos etc.

2. Correct your son if he makes sexist comments.

3. Ensure your son does housework on a regular basis and if you have daughters as well do not leave them to help around the house and let him off the hook.

Recommended Reading

Hip Hop Vs Maat: A Psycho/Social Analysis of Values
Culture Bandits Vols I & II – Del Jones

Freaks – Singers, Rappers, Actors and Athletes. The Role Modelling of Dysfunction

Introduction

How did we get to the situation where being able to fight, run fast, jump high, sing, dance or act, automatically made you a role model. This is the state of insanity we are living in. Several years ago I wrote an essay on this topic that was published in the now defunct Alarm magazine. Since that time things have got so much worse. The cult of celebrity which really started to grow dramatically in the 1980's has grown and blossomed into an ugly, poisonous cancer that is consuming the last vestiges of moral restraint in an increasingly amoral society.

We had 'Greed is Good' for Caucasians in the 1980's and now we have 'Get Rich or Die Trying' for Afrikans in the 2000's. It is incredible to look back and understand that when Marilyn Monroe, who was a Hollywood icon and definitely an 'A' List celebrity, died in the 1960's the report on her death in the New York Post appeared in the middle pages of the newspaper. She was not front page news. If she had lived today her death would have made the front pages of every single newspaper of note with multiple pages of coverage inside.

In the UK the biggest selling 'non-fiction' book for 2005 was the biography of Jordan, a topless model famous for exposing her large silicon filled breasts. Many talentless people are now becoming famous for no other reason than their desperate desire to become famous and their willingness to do almost anything to achieve fame.

It should be noted that this chapter is not about those Afrikans trying to promote positivity through their skill as Entertainers e.g. Mutabaruka, Public Enemy, Dead Prez, Arrested Development, Best Kept Secret, KRS1 etc., but rather those who have prostituted their talent to win fame and fortune from Europeans.

The impact of fame

So what I hear you ask. What has this got to do with saving our sons? Well, the issue is that of the role modelling of dysfunctional and in some cases deviant behaviour.

If you ask most Afrikan boys what they want to become when they grow up, it seems as if the majority want to be sportsmen, rappers, music producers or some sort of entertainer. When we look at the people who have 'made it' in those professions we have to have great concern that our sons do not come to believe that they should admire anything other than these people's talent in their respective fields, and certainly not wish to emulate their lifestyles.

Most Black athletes and entertainers are a complete waste of time when it comes to seeking to positively contribute to the upliftment of their people and modelling a positive Black conscious lifestyle. There are a few exceptions which only go to prove the rule. Famous people do not live by the same rules as ordinary folk. This has always been the case for powerful people whether they are famous or not. Fame tends to promote and create selfishness, arrogance, narcissism (vanity and self-obsession), sexual promiscuity and degeneracy, as well as insecurity –due to the fear of losing fame and status – amongst those who achieve it. As a rule of thumb, the greater the fame; the greater the tendency to manifest these characteristics.

The more famous a person becomes the more they are surrounded by people who tend to tell them what they want to hear as opposed to what they need to hear. Also, famous people tend to mix with other famous people and get drawn into a world of excess and unreality becoming divorced from the daily struggles of the majority of people in their country let alone the world.

The younger a person becomes famous the more likely that they will become psychologically troubled and dysfunctional as an adult. Judy Garland and Michael Jackson being two classic examples.

With the faces and imagery of these celebrities being pushed ever more frequently in front of our faces it is important to seriously consider how media commentators could even begin to suggest that these people should be role models on the basis of activity that has nothing to do with whether they engage in pro-social behaviour or not.

Let's take a few examples. In the early part of 2006 there were lurid newspaper articles about a homosexual orgy involving three Black Premiership footballers who were unnamed in the articles.

According to the reports of this episode, one of the footballers walked into the hotel room and said to the other two "so who is going to suck my dick then?" Later on one of the three put his mobile phone up his anus and asked one of the other two footballers to ring him so that him could experience the sensation of his phone vibrating in his anus. Role models?

Another Premiership footballer Sol Campbell, who has had allegations of homosexuality surrounding him for several years, disappeared after a game in early 2006. There were rumours that it was due to the break up of his relationship with a 45 year old Caucasian woman – he seems to specialise in dating unattractive, older White women – but there were also rumours that newspapers were going to break a story alleging that he was homosexual.

It is worth noting that of the well over 100 Black and Dual Heritage Premiership footballers, only one, to my knowledge, (Andrew Cole of Manchester City), has a Black or Dual Heritage partner. Role Models?

If we cross to the other side of the Atlantic, we have freaks such as R Kelly and Michael Jackson who are accepted as part of the Black community despite their record of sexual abuse. R Kelly who has a liking for sex with underage girls and apparently for urinating on them (something Chuck Berry was also into) was invited to perform by the Congressional Black Caucus (senior Black politicians in the US). Only a sick and degraded people would accept and promote a sexual degenerate such as R Kelly. Similarly, not only has Michael Jackson not been made an outcast by Afrikans in the US over his rejection of his Blackness, even when he went on to sexually abuse children he was not rejected. Is there anything that a Black person can do that would lead the Black community to reject them?

We have famous wifebeaters, rapists, drug addicts, paedophiles, homosexuals all being paraded as our role models. These people can do nothing more than teach us how to be good footballers, runners, dancers, rappers etc. Nothing more. Most have a talent, but it is not for right conduct.

When you think how much money these people earn and how little most of them invest in the development of our people you have to conclude that they are nothing more than clowns, jesters and buffoons who are dependent on their White Masters for endorsements, sponsorship deals and the White media coverage and support they crave and need to maintain their status. Remember, 'he who pays the Negro piper calls the tune'.

Lessons for Black Life

Question – There are around 4000 full-time professional athletes in the US and around 4000 neurosurgeons (brain surgeons). Why then do so many Afrikan boys in the US say they would like to be sportsmen when they grow up, but hardly any say they want to be brain surgeons?

Recommendations
For sons:
1. Do not chase fame. Fame may come to you depending upon your talents, however the likelihood is it will not. Afrikans who are desperate for fame inevitably sell Black people out.
2. Don't make celebrities your role models. You don't know what they are really like. Look for good responsible people who live in your local community.
For parents:
1. Discuss the values of celebrities with your son. Find out about the celebrities they are interested in, be they rap stars, footballers, basketball players etc.
2. Use the 1968 Mexico Olympics protest of Afrikan-American athletes (Tommy Smith, John Carlos, Lee Evans and others) as a basis to discuss the lack of consciousness of present day sports stars and celebrities. If you don't know about these events look it up on the internet or at the library.

Recommended Reading/Viewing

Bamboozled (DVD) – Spike Lee
Hollywood Shuffle (DVD) – Robert Townsend
Coach Carter (DVD)

100 points for killing a Black man – They kill Afrikans. Afrikan males and the Police

Christopher Alder – Death Stripped of Dignity
There follows below extracts from an article that appeared on the BBC News website with regard to the death in police custody of Christopher Alder, a 37 year old Afrikan man. Mr Alder died lying on the floor of a police station custody suite, handcuffed, with his trousers down around his knees, gasping for breath. He was left dying in that position for eleven minutes by four Caucasian police officers who made monkey noises whilst chatting. Christopher died of what they call 'positional asphyxia', that is to say he choked to death. Make sure you and your son learn the life and death lessons of Mr Alder's passing.
BBC News 14 April 2004

Dying man CCTV video is screened

The footage is described as 'very disturbing'
   CCTV footage of a former paratrooper choking to death while handcuffed and in police custody is to be shown in a BBC documentary.
   Christopher Alder, 37, of Hull, died at Queen's Gardens police station in Hull in April 1998.
   The father-of-two had been arrested in hospital, where he was being treated for a banged head following a scuffle outside a hotel.

Humberside Police had refused to release the footage.

The video will be shown as Mr Alder's sister Janet, of Burnley, Lancashire, calls for Home Secretary, David Blunkett, to order a public inquiry into her brother's death.

'Extreme measure'

She supports the programme-makers broadcasting the footage.

"It is an extreme measure, it has not been an easy decision to make but we feel that ordinary people need to know what's gone on," said Ms Alder.

"I'd like a public inquiry to make people aware of what is going on."
Janet Alder

10 *The Guardian* Wednesday April 14 2004

National news

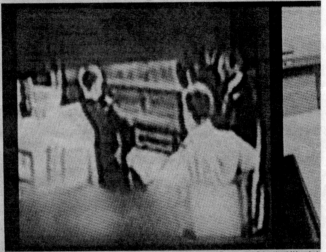

Left, CCTV footage of Christopher Alder on the floor of the police station and, right, a reconstruction. Below, Janet Alder, who is

TV to show dying minut

Family backs broadcast of CCTV footage revealing how ex-paratrooper c

Rosie Cowan
Crime correspondent

Shocking CCTV footage of a man dying on the floor of a police station surrounded by officers will be shown on prime-time television tonight in a bid to uncover the truth about his death.

Christopher Alder, a former paratrooper, died in Queens Gardens station in Hull on April 1 1998. His family, who want a full public inquiry, believe his death had racist overtones and was, at best, negligence and, at worst, manslaughter.

The black father-of-two was brought to the station from hospital after he became aggressive as he was treated for head injuries received in a fight outside a nightclub that night.

Tonight, for the first time, the public will get to view 11

harrowing minutes of CCTV recording. Mr Alder, who was 37, is seen and heard lying face down on the floor, his trousers round his knees, his breath rasping, and choking as he dies of a cardiac arrest. Officers accuse him of play acting and make no attempt to revive him.

Police refused to release the CCTV footage, but the documentary makers obtained a copy from another source.

Mr Alder's sister, Janet Alder, backed the decision to include the distressing scenes in the Rough Justice: Death on Camera documentary on BBC1 tonight. She hopes it will prove the final push in her family's long battle for justice.

"He spends his last 11 minutes on that floor, with no assistance whatsoever, with no dignity, no respect shown to him," she said. "I can't get my

head round the fact that we're living in a society where we're not safe in police custody."

Ms Alder is convinced the death had racist overtones, as are Mr Alder's two sons, Leon and Kevin, who were 13 and 15 when their father died.

In additional CCTV footage, seen by the BBC team but not included in the programme, monkey noises and laughter are heard as Mr Alder's dead body lies on the ground, where it remained for more than eight hours after his death, just before 4am.

In a statement released through their solicitor, Jane Deighton, Leon and Kevin Alder said: "Our family has lived with this agony for six years. Once again we ask for a public inquiry into our father's death. We need to know how and why he died. We need to know whether he died because

calling for a public inquiry into the death of her brother, pictured during his days as a paratrooper

es of man in custody

hoked on the floor as police did nothing to help

was black and whether ose responsible for his death ave escaped justice because was black."

At an inquest two years after Ir Alder's death, the jury, hich had seen the footage, corded a verdict of unlawful lling. But the Crown Prosecu-on Service decided that there as not enough evidence to cing a case against the five umberside police officers pre-nt when he died.

Nigel Dawson, Neil Blakey, hn Dunn, Matthew Barr and lark Ellerington refused to nswer questions put to them the inquest. The Alder fam-y sought out independent edical experts and eventually he police officers were harged over the death, but the dge ruled there was no case to nswer. An internal disciplinary earing cleared them of

with the Humberside force. Four are on sick leave, while the fifth has made a partial return to work.

Steve Love, the Humberside deputy chief constable, told the BBC he could not com-ment on police actions the night Mr Alder died because civil proceedings were ongo-ing. The police position has al-ways been that the officers had no idea how serious Mr Alder's injuries were.

West Yorkshire police car-ried out an investigation into the death. But the family are

'He spends his last 11 minutes on that floor, with … no respect shown to him'

still demanding to be told why blood was wiped from the po-lice van, and why the officers' clothes were dry-cleaned and Mr Alder's destroyed before full forensic tests could be car-ried out.

The family also want to know why he had to be dragged unconscious into the police station when he was able to walk to the police van minutes before and why he was left suffering when he ob-viously needed medical help.

They are backed by Inquest, which monitors deaths in cus-tody, and Liberty, which is tak-ing the case to the the Euro-pean court of human rights.

Helen Shaw, of Inquest, said the CCTV footage of Mr Alder's death was the most distressing thing she had seen. He is one of 200 black people who have died in UK police or prison

Two medical experts believe Mr Alder died of neglect. Jack Crane, the Northern Ireland state pathologist, said it was not unusual for people with head injuries to become ag-gressive. Mr Alder had sus-tained two severe blows out-side the Waterfront nightclub in Hull before becoming aggressive at the hospital.

"I still do not have any doubts that his death, when it occurred, was due to the lack of attention he got when he was brought into the police station." Prof Crane said.

Nat Cary, a Home Office pathologist and a lead expert witness at the Soham murder trial, said Mr Alder could have survived if basic medical pro-cedures had been observed, such as putting him in the recovery position and making sure that his airways were clear

Following eight years of tireless campaigning, Janet Alder was able to get an enquiry into Christopher's death by the IPCC (Independent Police Complaints Commission) although this was not the public enquiry that Ms Alder wanted and is still fighting for.

There follows some extracts from the Executive Summary of this report, which ran to some 409 pages, with my comments/ interpretations in bold:

"His last minutes of life were captured on CCTV. They are shocking and distressing pictures." (page 9)

There is no doubt in my mind that the events leading to and following Mr Alder's death represent very serious failings by many of the individuals and organisations involved..." (page 10)

This is the same old story we heard after the Stephen Lawrence enquiry and after the death of Anthony Mensa. They always conclude that this can never be allowed to happen again and it always does.

"...all the experts agreed that, at the very least, the officers' neglect undoubtedly did deny him the chance of life." (page 10)

As usual the officers were cleared of criminal charges. It is almost impossible to secure a conviction for murder, manslaughter or other serious assault against a police officer for actions carried out whilst on duty. This is the same worldwide and especially in places where White police officers confront young Afrikan men. In Brazil killing young brothers has almost become a national sport for police officers (check out the film 'City of God')

"If the lack of common sense and common decency displayed by the officers who watched Mr Alder die is typical of how any police officer would react, it is a disturbing comment on the police service as a whole." I do not believe this is the case....their behaviour has disgraced police officers and the police service as a whole." (page 11)

This is what they call the 'rotten apples' explanation where they claim these officers are untypical and represent a few rotten apples in the barrel. However remember what happens if you leave rotten apples in a barrel? They infect the whole barrel!

"I believe the failure of the police officers concerned to assist Mr Alder effectively on the night he died was largely due to assumptions they made about him based on negative racial stereotypes. Lord

Macpherson describes this as 'unwitting racism' and I believe his analysis and many of his recommendations are directly relevant to this case." (page 12)

Please understand this is White liberal, handwringing foolishness. They are trying to say that they were racist but didn't know that they were racist, so it's not so bad is it! The police officers were heard making monkey noises and referring to 'banana boats' both before and after Christopher Alder's death. If this is 'unwitting racism' what is witting racism? They left him to die because in their eyes he was a n*g*er monkey. They would have treated a dog with more care. Let us deal with the harsh reality and not believe the excuses made up for each other by our enemies.

Learning for Afrikan Life

1. Afrikan men are massively over-represented amongst those people killed by police officers in the line of duty on the streets, and in police custody and prison. This is the same in all the White dominated countries across the world. Why do you think this is?
2. Does your son know what to do if stopped by the police? Does he know his legal rights? If not, find out as a priority.
3. Role play the police stopping your son and trying to wind him up.
4. Black life is viewed as cheap all over the world. If your son does not value his life not many others will.
5. It does not matter how many Black police or prison officers there are in 'majority White' countries, it will never stop the killing and abuse of Afrikans.
6. Should Afrikan men join the Police Force? Discuss this with your son. Personally I would never join a Caucasian Police Force or Armed Service and I would actively discourage my son (and daughter) from doing so. If you can get hold of the two 'Dispatches' programmes aired on Channel 4 (UK) which investigated police conduct using undercover reporters you will know why. This is not to condemn all Afrikan police officers, some are conscious brothers and sisters, however in my experience the

majority are not. Remember, Afrikans cannot change Caucasian institutions. At best you survive them. Also remember that Christopher Alder had fought for 'his country' and this still meant nothing as he was left to die.

Recommended Reading/Viewing

Eyes To My Soul: The Rise and Decline of a Black FBI Agent – Tyrone Powers
Boyz in the Hood (DVD)
Dispatches: Undercover Copper – Channel 4 (27 April 2006)

Suicide by any other name – Afrikan youth killing each other

In reflecting upon the perception and sometimes reality of young Afrikan males as menaces to their own society and the contrast in how some other communities in the US view their men, Jawanza Kunjufu says:

"If a Black woman was walking down the street late at night by herself and someone was walking toward her, she would probably hope that the person walking toward her be a Black woman first, a White woman second, a White male third and the Black male last. Black men send fear in the hearts of Black women. An Italian woman in Little Italy would hope to see an Italian man, first, an Italian woman second, a Black woman third, and the Black male never. An Italian woman in Little Italy desires an Italian man first; a Black woman in the Black community desires a Black man last. I believe when African American women will prefer African American men first our liberation from white supremacy will be achieved." (Kunjufu 1995: 50)

N.B. Little Italy is a working class Italian-American community in Baltimore, USA.

Dr Kunjufu goes on to say:

"A people without their culture will be afraid to walk down the street at three o'clock in the morning and meet someone who looks like them because they can never be sure whether they share the same value system. A people without a culture and values are dangerous. (Kunjufu 1995: 51)

The latter quote highlights the point I made earlier, in the chapter on parenting, about values as the foundation of parenting. Dr Kunjufu hits the nail on the head. We are a people without our culture, which is not the same thing as to say that we are a people without culture, it is just that most of us are living in the wrong culture. It is the cultural plague of 'Niggeritis' (see Introduction) that leads young Afrikans to destroy other Afrikans for the right to sell drugs to other Afrikans, as a matter of 'respect', or over a woman whom they view as their property.

As Professor Wade Nobles puts it, "Culture is to people as water is to fish, invisible, pervasive and essential."

Given the systematic brutalisation and war waged by Whites against Blacks the question has been asked 'Why don't Afrikan men kill Caucasian men in far greater numbers?' For me there are a few main reasons:

1. Subconscious Fear – The penalty for an Afrikan killing a Caucasian is more severe than if the Afrikan kills another Afrikan and the chances of getting caught are much greater. An Afrikan man killing a Caucasian man in the US is up to **six times** more likely to get the death penalty than a Caucasian man killing an Afrikan man.

2. Psychological conditioning – All people are conditioned to believe that White lives have more value than non-White lives and that Afrikan lives have the lowest value of all. The media play a major role in this e.g. the initial report on Stephen Lawrence's murder appeared as a small column piece way back in the middle pages of the Daily Mail newspaper when he was murdered. The front page lead story was about a young blonde Caucasian woman from Essex who was murdered. The Daily Mail only picked up the story later on because Stephen Lawrence's father decorated the editor's house!

3. Proximity and Acquaintances – In most cases people are murdered by someone from the same ethnic group. Most murders involve the victim being killed by someone they know.

Unless our youth receive structured cultural training and indoctrination they will continue to vent their pent up anger and frustration on their own people, proving that murder can also be suicide in all but name.

In terms of the more traditional view of suicide, in May 2006 I was listening to a recording of a presentation by Dr Asa Hilliard on an internet radio station www.innerlightradio.com . I am not sure when the presentation was recorded, however it was probably in the last few years. During his presentation Dr Hilliard discussed the issue of suicide amongst young Afrikan people in the United States. After

noting that traditionally suicide was virtually unknown in Afrika –
and that even after our kidnapping, terrorisation and enslavement in
'the West' suicide rates were still extremely low – Dr Hilliard noted
the dramatically increasing suicide rates amongst young Afrikans. He
noted that suicide was one of the main causes of death amongst
young Afrikans aged 15-20 in the USA and that the suicide rate for
Afrikans aged 10-14 had increased by 300% in recent years.

Dr Hilliard mentioned a research project examining suicides
amongst young Afrikans that he had provided professional advice to.
He said that the research identified two key common factors amongst
the young Afrikan people who had attempted suicide. These were:

1. Their families had not taught them how to deal with a racist
   society and therefore they were ill-equipped to deal with set-backs
   and hostility which were due to racism.
2. These young people did not belong to anything e.g. religious
   organisations, youth groups, clubs or societies, even gangs. They
   were socially isolated.

It is interesting that these two factors, more than any issue to do with
unemployment, educational failure etc. were the most likely
indicators of suicide amongst young Afrikans in the USA.

Suicide, Abortion and Murder

Just as Afrikans have adopted the alien value and practice of suicide
so we have come to adopt the alien value and practice of abortion
which is now so common it has come to be viewed by many as
nothing more than a form of delayed birth control. It has been
estimated that since the 1960's over 18 million Afrikan babies (nearly
equivalent to half the current Afrikan population in the US) have been
aborted by Black women in the USA. Think what difference those 18
odd million Afrikans could have made to Afrikan empowerment as
we look at a situation where so-called Hispanics are now about to
overtake Afrikans as the largest minority group in the USA. Afrikan
women in the US make up 12% of the female population but have
34% of all abortions.

This is due to the deliberate and successful attempt by the US government, by means of social policy, to suppress Afrikan fertility by changing our people's value system and destroying the Afrikan family. This is similar to how homosexuality is being promoted amongst Afrikans. If you don't believe me go back to the quote by Margaret Sanger, a noted eugenicist (eugenics is the 'science' of improving the genetic make-up of a given population by encouraging those considered to have desirable genes to breed and just as importantly, discouraging those with undesirable genes [i.e. Afrikans and so-called 'White Trash'] from breeding) and population control advocate at the beginning of this book.

In the UK we see a similar trend in suicides, murder and abortion amongst Afrikans. In the 1990's I met an Afrikan young woman who was quite open about the fact that she had had three abortions before the age of 20. There was no pretence that there was any other motivation other than the fact that she didn't want to have a child at the time.

So you see that Afrikan life is being destroyed and denied at every turn whilst governments in countries such as Portugal and Germany are offering financial incentives for the women of their countries to produce more White babies. The collusion of Afrikans in this destruction of Black life has been achieved by promoting the development of an anti-Afrikan, anti-life value system in our people which has led to the belief that there is nothing cheaper than an Afrikan life. Finally, the push towards the acceptance of euthanasia is another part of the European culture of death. So there you have it, death at the beginning of life (abortion) death at the end of life (euthanasia) and death in between (suicide and murder).

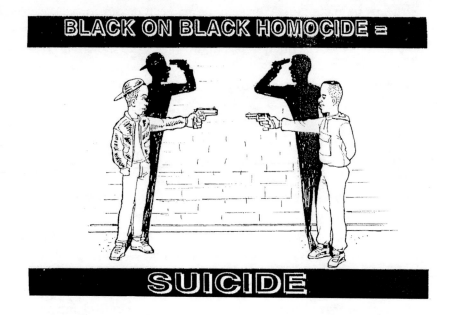

The Purpose of Gangs

Every human activity has a purpose, whether that purpose is consciously or unconsciously recognised, or whether it serves a pro-social or anti-social purpose, and so it is with gangs. In every country you go to you will see that young people, and young males in particular, like to hang out together in groups. These groups are labelled as gangs when their activities are deemed anti-social or when their members are mainly from an 'outgroup' in that particular society. And there is no bigger outgroup in the Caucasian world than young Afrikan males.

So what is the purpose of gangs for our sons? Well, gangs provide:

- A sense of identity
- Social status and recognition amongst one's peer group and sometimes in the wider community
- Protection against other gangs
- A role and sense of purpose
- Friendship and loyalty
- A sense of family and kinship

- A means to make money or acquire material possessions
- An outlet for aggressive impulses
- Older role models often referred to as OG's (substitute father figures)
- Excitement and adrenalin rush
- Male Leadership
- Access to sexually active females i.e. crewbangers

As you can see, virtually all of the needs satisfied by gangs are legitimate, it is how these needs are met that can be criminal or anti-social. In the final analysis gangs are like surrogate families. Gang members always have time for each other, whereas busy parents often do not. Gangs provide plenty of (anti-social) male role models whereas many Black communities do not. Gangs are our sons' way of telling us that they need male leadership, direction, quality time, attention, friendship, Love and purpose.

We have to learn from gangs and provide our young men with positive male groups to join and identify with. The needs that the gangs meet we must meet (apart from providing crewbangers!), but in a positive pro-social context.

It should be noted that I have been told by an absolutely trustworthy source that there are three unreformed, hard core gangbangers from the US who are on **parole** and yet have been allowed into the UK. You need to realise that there is no way that these individuals could have been allowed to leave the US and enter into the UK without the collusion of the US government. The parole conditions imposed on serious offenders in the US – particularly gang members – are extremely strict. You can imagine the mayhem these people are going to cause in the UK as they build links between US gangs and UK gangs.

Lesson – **The Enemy Never Sleeps.**

In conclusion we can ask?

"It would be interesting to study if there's any connection between Blacks being forced to inflict punishment on one another and today's Black on Black crime. Can there be any deep rooted hatred ingrained in our sub-conscious mind? Or is it that European savagery has rubbed off on us."

Nana Wkow Butweiku I 500 Years of European Behavior

Questions for Parents to ask Sons:

1. Ask your son to list all the reasons he would be prepared to use violence against another person, then ask him to list all the reasons he thinks people could legitimately use violence against him.
2. Ask your son if he has been involved in any violent confrontations – particularly involving bats, sticks, knives, guns or other weapons – with other Afrikan youth and to describe the events leading up to the violence. What could he have done differently to avoid the violence?
3. Ask your son if he is a member of a gang and if so why.

Recommendations

For parents:

1. Discuss depictions of 'Black-on-Black violence in the media with your son.
2. If one does not already exist, encourage the men in your community to set up a rites of passage programme and get your son on it.
3. Insist that your stable adult male relatives spend time with your son.
4. Go through the list of needs that gangs meet and identify how you can ensure these needs are being met positively in your son's life.

For sons:

1. Remember, violence begets violence so always use violence as a last resort.
2. Don't move with people who disrespect Afrikans, verbally or physically.
3. Learn how to control your temper and your mind. Self-control is important, especially when under threat.

Recommended Reading/Viewing

Understanding Black Adolescent Male Violence – Amos N Wilson
Black on Black Violence – Amos N Wilson
Countering the Conspiracy to Destroy Black Boys Vols I-IV

Where have all the soldiers gone?

'Two bull can't reign in one pen.'
Jamaican proverb

Introduction

The above Jamaican proverb highlights the relationship between father and son and the fact that at the appropriate time the son must leave his parent's home to establish himself as a man and become architect of his own destiny. If a man stays too long in the parental home he will become stifled and will stop developing. If he departs too soon he will be unprepared for life and risks making many unnecessary mistakes as he learns by trial and error. However we live in strange times and instead of sons leaving the parental home it is the fathers who are leaving (if they were around in the first place).

Afrikan men – Missing in Action or AWOL (Absent Without Leave)

When a soldier is **missing in action** his status is indeterminate i.e. people don't know whether he has been killed, injured or captured.

When a soldier has gone **AWOL** he has left the battlefield or barracks without permission from a commanding officer. If it is a time of war he is labelled a deserter.

When a soldier leaves the battlefield due to psychological trauma this is described as '**Shell Shock**' (Post-Traumatic Stress Disorder).

When a soldier leaves the battlefield or refuses to carry out an order out of fear he is labelled a **coward**.

When a soldier refuses to fight because of moral objections he is labelled a **Conscientious Objector**.

When a soldier is secretly working for the enemy he is deemed a traitor.

Deserters, Cowards and Traitors face the death penalty during times of war. Conscientious Objectors face imprisonment. The Shell Shocked, if diagnosed, will receive treatment and counselling to help them overcome their trauma. Those who are missing in action are memorialised.

This is a time of war, so let us look at these different types of soldier in our community.

Missing in Action

There are many brothers missing in action. These are brothers who have been killed or injured as part of their struggle against White oppression. Some of these brothers have suffered psychological injuries which have left them incapacitated and lost, but unnoticed and therefore they do not receive any support or treatment from Afrikan people as they limp along unseen and unnoticed.

AWOL

These are brothers who have abandoned their girlfriends/wives, children and community responsibilities in favour of a life of 'prolonged adolescence'. They want fast cars, faster women, intoxicating substances and a collection of toys. They are males not men whatever their physical strength or prowess. Some of these brothers don't know any better and are simply repeating the cycle of their own troubled upbringing. Others know better, but do not care, choosing to live a life of me, myself and I. They all suffer from arrested psychological development.

Shell Shock (Post-Traumatic Stress Disorder)

These brothers have been seriously psychologically injured and will probably never return to the battlefield. They may receive little sympathy due to people's attitude to psychological as opposed to physical illness. Childhood emotional, physical or sexual abuse, adult rape or other forms of traumatic experience can psychologically disable the brother. Given the generally high levels of mental illness in many Afrikan communities these brothers often get lost in the crowd. I believe it was Dr Patricia Newton who first coined the term 'Post-Traumatic Slavery Disorder' and Dr Joy DeGruy Leary has published a book entitled 'Post-Traumatic Slave Syndrome'. Both speak to our collective distress as people too often locked in psychological bondage.

Cowards

Cowards often turn into traitors, since like water they will always choose the path of least resistance. It is said that 'a coward dies a thousand times but a brave man only once', since doing that which you know to be wrong, out of fear, has a corrosive effect. It gnaws away at your heart and mind. It brings a sense of shame and guilt since cowards essentially are not against Afrikan people, they just fear the consequences of fighting for Afrikan people. Cowards will **always** suggest caution, **always** want White approval before embarking upon any new course of action, **never** speak out in front of Caucasians or Negroes who could damage their career prospects etc. but often act very differently in private.

Conscientious Objectors

In the battle against the ideology and practice of White Supremacy the Conscientious Objectors are pacifists who believe that we shall overcome with love, the meek shall inherit the Earth, turn the other cheek, brotherhood of man, love thine enemy etc. Let's be clear, I am not talking about Christians as a whole, although many of these Conscientious Objectors have internalised White Christianity. Many of our most fierce fighters were Christians e.g. Rev. Sam Sharpe, Rev. Nat Turner, David Walker, Marcus Mosiah Garvey etc. who did not let some of the rhetoric of their religion stand in the way of fighting for our people.

No sensible people adopt non-violence as a group philosophy. Non-violence is a tactic not a viable group philosophy in a world full of hostile groups prepared to use violence against you. In any case, most of these Conscientious Objectors are hypocrites. If you put them in a situation where their family members were about to raped and killed by a brutal psychopath you would see how quickly their hand would reach for rock, knife, stick etc. As our great ancestor David Walker said:

"Now, I ask you, had you not rather be killed than to be a slave to a tyrant, who takes the life of your mother, wife, and dear little children? Look upon your mother, wife and children, and answer God Almighty; and believe this, that it is no more harm for you to kill a man, who is trying to kill you, than it is for you to take a drink of water when thirsty; in fact, the man who will stand still and let another murder him, is worse than an infidel, and, if he has common sense, ought not be pitied."

Traitors

These dogs deserve no sympathy or kindness. These are people who are consciously and actively selling out Afrikan people because Caucasians have the upper hand. They have no conscience and there are more rewards available from siding with what they see as the winning team. Traitors will sell us out for money, fame, status, sex or anything else they value. They can always rationalise their treachery and Caucasians always put them forward when they want to attack Afrikans since they know that some of our people are gullible enough to give these people a hearing despite their track record of selling us out. Traitors are normally very bright, which is why Caucasians use them, hence they are able to make their anti-Afrikan behaviour sound reasonable. Two obvious examples are Colin Powell and Trevor Phillips.

Conclusion

As Afrikan men we all have different skills, personalities and roles to play in our people's struggle for liberation, however there is no excuse for not making some contribution to that struggle unless you are severely ill or impaired. I am making my contribution as an information soldier, fighting on the battlefield of ideas. Using words as my weapons of mass upliftment to help us all see a better day. What are you doing?

Recommended Reading/Viewing

Asafo: A Warrior's Guide to Manhood – Mwalimu K Bomani Baruti
Showdown – Del Jones

Success is your Birthright

"When the fool learns the game the players have dispersed."
Ashanti proverb

What is Success?
Here is a simple definition to get you started.

"Success is the continuous realisation of the outcomes
or results you desire."
Herbert Harris

The Success Triangle

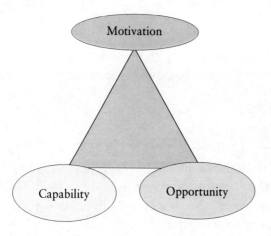

The above diagram shows the three essential components for success.

Capability – Do you have the knowledge, skills and experience to successfully pursue your goals? You can develop your capability with study, observation (watching people) and hard work (practice).

Opportunity – Is the chance there to use your skills in the way you want? There has never been more opportunity for a young Afrikan if you have your head screwed on the right way.

Motivation – Do you really want it? You must want success so badly that you can taste it!

The biggest problem most young Afrikan men have is not lack of opportunity, or even lack of capability, because with hard work you can develop your skills and knowledge. No, it is that White Racism is destroying your Motivation. Remember:

'You may not be responsible for getting knocked down, but you are responsible for getting up.'

So, get off your arse, stop moaning and start succeeding!

The Truth about Success

Understand that success does not happen by chance. There are rules to being successful just as there are rules to a game of football or basketball.

"You become what you think about most of the time."
Earl Nightingale

Some Simple Tips

Be Constant in your efforts – Everyone loves a trier. Just keep on keeping on and you will get there in the end.

Get Away from the Crowd at the Bottom – Birds of a feather flock together. If you want to fly you need to move with the eagles not scratch around with the chickens. Check out your friends and honestly assess whether they are focused on success.

Be Willing to Change – If you keep on doing the same thing you will always get the same result. You know you can do even better, so get on with it!

Nine Rules for becoming a success

- Do not procrastinate (delay) – procrastination is suicide by instalments
- Do it now – There is always something you can do today to build success
- Stand on your own two feet – Stop blaming others and take

116

personal responsibility for your own actions

- Do not fear failure – "My life has been filled with terrible misfortunes, most of which never happened." Montaigne (French writer)
- Do not sell yourself cheaply – If you value yourself there is a good chance that others will value you also
- Develop the success habit of being goal oriented – Targets should be realistic but challenging
- Visualise your goals and believe you can attain them – If you don't believe in yourself who is going to believe in you?
- Plan your work, and work your plan – People don't plan to fail they fail to plan
- Do not give up – If at first you don't succeed, then try; try again

When you get to the end of your rope,
Tie a knot and hang on.
Be prepared to do whatever it takes,
For as long as it takes.

The Twelve Laws of Success

I.   Law of Thought – You are what you think
II.   Law of Change – Faith, Choice and Desire – Change is natural and if you change your thinking you can change your life
III. Law of Vision – Specificity and Imagination – A people without vision shall perish. Your vision must be crystal clear.
IV.   The Law of Affirmation – Positive sayings can help you to think positively e.g. 'Everyday in every way I am getting better and better'
V.   The Law of Magnetism – Like attracts like – Birds of a feather flock together
VI.   The Law of Focus and Discipline – What you recognise, you energise, What you energise you realise
VII. The Law of Action – Hard work is essential (Success is 99% perspiration, 1% inspiration)
VIII. The Law of Value and Mutual Exchange – Do not waste your

time, thoughts, actions and money

IX. The Law of Relationships – Sort out your relationship with The Creator, Yourself, Others, Material things and the Environment

X. The Law of Supply and Opportunity – Everything you need is available in abundance. Opportunity is infinite

XI. The law of Persistence – If you persist in doing the right things you will get the right results

XII. The Law of Truth – The truth may sometimes hurt, but the truth will set you free

How to Set Goals

There are three types of goal – short-term (1-90 days), medium term (90 days – 3 years depending upon age), long-term (3 years-lifetime)

Ingredients of a goal

- It should be written, committed to and shared.
- It should be realistic and attainable
- It should challenging and specific
- It should be flexible and reflect change
- It should be concrete and measurable
- It should be extended to cover certain time periods
- It should be set in advance!

'Everyday in every way I'm getting better and better.'

'Every day do your best and every day make your best better.'
(Paul Grant)

Recommendations
For sons:

For sons:

1. If you don't have a plan, write one with clear goals. Read the plan every day for the first 30 days so that it gets fixed in your head.
2. Share the plan with your parents and put it up on your bedroom wall.
3. Speak to your friends about what they dream of accomplishing. Encourage them to believe in themselves.
4. Remember, an ambition without a plan is just a Dream.
5. Stop being afraid of failure. Everyone experiences failure and negative events. The key is how you deal with these.
6. You need to decide if you want to be a sheep or a shepherd!

For parents:

1. 'For things to Change we have to change.' What are you doing to improve yourself?
2. Draw up a lifeplan for yourself and show it to your son. When he sees you practicing what you preach he will step up. Put your lifeplan up on your bedroom wall.

Books to read if you are serious about success

- The Twelve Universal Laws of Success – Herbert Harris
- If Caterpillars Can Fly So Can I – Alvin Day
- The Seven Habits of Highly Successful People – Stephen R. Covey
- Think and Grow Rich a Black Choice – Dennis Kimbro

Much of the information in this chapter is adapted from Herbert Harris' excellent book 'The Twelve Universal Laws of Success' (2005) published by the LifeSkill Institute.

Endnote

"Those who want dignity must pay for it in the proper currency –
power."
Chinweizu – The West and the Rest of Us

We are a people at war, however only one side is waging war.

Most Afrikans don't like to hear this sort of talk. They think it is dangerous and radical, however there is nothing more dangerous for a people than sleepwalking to disaster. We are being funnelled over the edge of a cliff and our Negro leaders are encouraging us to form an orderly queue!

Look around the world and the generally terrible condition of Afrikan people. Everywhere you look we are at the bottom of the social, economic, educational, political, religious and cultural pile. Is this natural? Is this the way it is meant to be? If you believe the answer is yes, perhaps you need put the chip back into the base of your skull, plug back into the Matrix and go and sit down and watch TV!

If you believe the answer is no, then the question for all of us is: What are we going to do about it?

There is a war going on and Afrikan men and boys are in the frontline. Loving your enemy when they are trying to destroy you will put you in your grave, fast.

White Supremacy or White racism changes in the tactics used but essentially remains the same. The Afrikan family was attacked under slavery, attacked under colonialism and is still being attacked under neo-colonialism. Family is the key to a people's strength. There is an Akan proverb which says that the ruin of a nation will begin in its homes, which is a clear indication that our ancestors understood the importance of family.

When men wage war they take out the opposition men first and then the women and children bear the brunt of the assault. Well, Caucasian men have conquered Afrikan men and now they are coming for Afrikan women and children. Too many Afrikan men are reduced to helplessness by prison, mental illness, alcohol, other drugs, arrested emotional development, sex obsession, ghetto fabulous lifestyle etc. However Caucasian men know that in every Afrikan generation the seeds of Afrikan liberation flower and bloom again, so the plan is to destroy Afrikan men whilst they are boys! Our boys are in peril. Caucasians want to hold onto their power and wealth which has been gained through genocide against Afrikans and other peoples around the world. We need to **take** power from them, hence conflict is inevitable until there is justice.

Kush the Unifier tells us that there are four types of Negro in the world: The Stupid, The Confused, The Scared and The Traitorous Uncle Toms (and Aunt Jemimas). All of them are dangerous and will sell out Afrikan people for anything from a job, status, fame or a White woman. Our job is to make sure our sons do not become these people and bring shame to our names. We can start by making sure we are not these kinds of people ourselves!

Our boys' purpose should not be to get a good job. It should be to find a constructive way to contribute to the liberation of Afrikan people. A job should be a means to an end not an end in itself and if it is not a vocation, such as being a doctor, physicist, lawyer, sculptor etc. it should be viewed as preparation for self-employment. The job of Afrikan adults is to sort our mess out so that we can prepare the next generation for the struggles ahead.

Thank you for reading this book. However the best way you can thank me for writing it is to work with your son, or mother/father, to implement the ideas it contains, so that we can all see a better day.

"The god who created the sun which gives us light, who rouses the waves and rules the storm, though hidden in the clouds, he watches us. He sees all that the white man does. The god of the white man inspires him with crime, but our god calls upon us to do good works. Our god who is good to us orders us to revenge our wrongs. He will direct our arms and aid us. Throw away the symbol of the god of the whites who has so often caused us to weep, and listen to the voice of liberty, which speaks in the hearts of us all."

Bookman Dutty
(Prime catalyst for the Haitian revolution), 1791

Tendai Mwari (Unto the Creator be Thankful)

Bibliography

Anderson, C. (2001) Powernomics – The National Plan to Empower Black America, Bethesda, Maryland: Powernomics Corporation of America

Baruti, K.B. (2003) HOMOSEXUALITY AND THE EFFEMINZATION OF AFRIKAN MALES, Atlanta, Georgia: Akoben House

BBC News 14 April 2004, Dying Man CCTV Video Footage is screened, www.bbc.co.uk

Berthoud, R. (2006) Family formation in multi-cultural Britain: three patterns of diversity, University of Essex: Institute for Social and Economic Research

Black Hair and Beauty Magazine Dec 2004/Jan 2005

Eckholm, E (2006) 'Plight Deepens for Black Men, Statistics Warns', New York Times

Eke, C. 23 February 2006, Young black men are victims of 'statistical racism', www.blackbritain.co.uk

Grant, P. (2003) Niggers, Negroes, Black People and Afrikans, Nottingham, United Kingdom: Navig8or Press

Grant, P. (2005) Blue Skies for Afrikans, Nottingham, United Kingdom: Navig8or Press

Guardian Newspaper, page 10, 14 April 2004, London and Manchester, Guardian Newspapers Ltd.

Hare, N. and Hare, J. (1991) The Hare Plan, To Overhaul the Public Schools and Educate Every Black Man, Woman and Child, San Francisco, Cal: BLACK THINK TANK

Hare, N. and Hare, J. (1993) The Endangered Black Family: Coping with the Unisexualisation and Coming Extinction of the Black Race, San Francisco, CA,: BLACK THINK TANK

Harris, H. (2005) The Twelve Universal Laws of Success, Wilmington, North Carolina: The LifeSkill Institute Inc.

Kunjufu, J. (1995) Countering the Conspiracy to Destroy Black Boys Volume Four, Chicago, Illinois: African American Images

Kunjufu, J. (2001) Hip-Hop vs. MAAT: A Psycho/Social Analysis of Values, Chicago, Illinois: African American Images

Nobles, W.W. (1990's) Education of the Black Child Conference, Manchester

One City Partnership Nottingham, (2005) Action From Facts: Educational Attainment, Focus on Black Boys, (Unpublished)

Report dated 27th February 2006, of the Review into the events leading up to and following the death of Christopher Alder on 1st April 1998 by the Independent Police Complaints Commission

Staples, R. (1989) 'Beauty and the Beast: The Importance of Physical Attractiveness in the Black Community' in Hare, N. and Hare, J. (Eds) (1989) CRISIS IN BLACK SEXUAL POLITICS, San Francisco, Cal: BLACK THINK TANK

Walker, D. (1995) David Walker's APPEAL – To the COLOURED CITIZENS OF THE WORLD, but in particular, and very expressly, to those of THE UNITED STATES OF AMERICA, New York: Hill and Wang

Wilson-Eme, P.O. Recommendations for Parents (Unpublished)

Wright, B.E. (1984) THE PSYCHOPATHIC RACIAL PERSONALITY: AND OTHER ESSAYS, Chicago: Third World Press

Wilson, A.N. (1987) The Developmental Psychology of The Black Child, New York: Africana Research Publications

Wilson, A.N. (1991) Understanding Black Adolescent Male Violence: Its Remediation and Prevention, New York: AFRIKAN WORLD INFOSYSTEMS

Appendix 1 – Action Plan for Change (Example in Red)

Objective	Tasks/Actions	Who needs to do it	Resources e.g. Time, Money, Equipment	Target Date	Actual Date Achieved
To get at least 70% in end of year Maths test (up from 60%)	- To always arrive on time to Maths lessons. - To sit in front three rows in class - To ask teacher to explain homework if I don't understand - To start homework on the day I receive it - To get home tuition	Leon Leon Leon Leon Mum to arrange	Time Money to pay for tuition	End of School Year exams in June	

About The Author

Paul Ifayomi Grant was born in Edmonton, North London, in 1966, the second of three children. He was schooled in Edmonton and Enfield until the age of 18. He has worked in a variety of roles in the Midlands, including running his own recruitment consultancy business, working in prisons and with ex-offenders as an Employment/Training Adviser, working as a Training & Development Manager, Community Safety Consultant and most recently as the Deputy Chief Executive of a multi-million pound neighbourhood regeneration programme where he had overall responsibility for project delivery, partnership working and Human Resource issues. In February 2006 Ifayomi completed the circle and returned to self-employment and he now works as a writer as well as operating his own consultancy firm Navigation Consulting Ltd.

He is an active member of the Afrikan community in Nottingham and is involved in a number of community groups, most notably: Nubian Link a community education group, ABDF Ltd (formerly Afrikan Business Development Fund) a community economic development company which he conceived and co-founded, Vice-Chair and co-founder of the Nottingham Black Families in Education Parent Support Group which provides educational advocacy and support, a founder member of Brother II Brother an Afrikan men's group delivering rites of passage programmes, and a founder member of the Afrikan Education Forum. Paul also helped to create the Empower Group, a support group for Afrikans working in mentoring, which over time has transformed to become a group of friends who support each other on their life journeys.

Paul is the son of Orinthea and Reuben Grant. He is married to a beautiful Afrikan queen Beverley and they have two lovely children Jawanza Kwesi and Abiba Ashia Orinthea. He has an elder brother Nigel and a younger sister Tracey.

To contact the author please email him at: ifayomi@ntlworld.com

Visit his website where you can buy his books online, subscribe to his free newsletter and read unpublished essays by the author: www.houseofknowledge.org.uk

Or telephone Hotep Communications on 07977 495425

If you would like to enquire about the author's consultancy services please contact Navigation Consulting Ltd. on (0115) 9109835 or email him at the address above.

Other Books by Paul Ifayomi Grant

Niggers, Negroes, Black People and Afrikans

Blue Skies for Afrikans

Sankofa the Wise Man and his Amazing Friends